Royal
Horticultural
Society

TAKE CHELSEA HOME

Royal
Horticultural
Society

TAKE CHELSEA HOME

Practical inspiration from
the RHS Chelsea Flower Show

Written by **CHRIS YOUNG**

Foreword by **Alan Titchmarsh**

MITCHELL BEAZLEY

For my wife Nikki, and children Jacob and Isabella, whose
bedtime was always followed by 'Daddy's book'

First published in Great Britain in 2010 by Mitchell Beazley,
an imprint of Octopus Publishing Group Ltd,
Endeavour House, 189 Shaftesbury Avenue, London
WC2H 8JG
www.octopusbooks.co.uk

An Hachette UK Company
www.hachette.co.uk

Published by Mitchell Beazley, an imprint of the
Octopus Publishing Group in association with
The Royal Horticultural Society.

ISBN: 978 1 84533 538 0

A CIP record for this book is available from the British Library.
Colour reproduction by Fine Arts
Printed and bound in China by Toppan

Commissioning Editor Helen Griffin
Editor Joanne Wilson
Copy-editor Joanna Chisholm
Proofreader Lynn Bresler
Technical Consultant Andrew Wilson
Indexer Diana LeCore
Art Director Pene Parker
Senior Art Editor Juliette Norsworthy
Designer Lizzie Ballantyne
Design Co-ordinator Gary Almond
Picture Research Manager Giulia Hetherington
Production Controller Peter Hunt

CONTENTS

Foreword   6
Introduction   10

Chelsea Style   16
Entrances, Paths and Boundaries   26
Planting   50
Outdoor Living   80
Water   104
Materials   130
Sustainability   152
Productive Gardens   174
Lighting   188
Art in the Garden   202

Index of gardens and designers   218
Index   220
Acknowledgements   224

[previous page] A view into the world of the RHS Chelsea Flower Show. Creativity and imagination combine to give endless ideas for the home gardener. Here flat 'slabs' of water are framed by tall tree ferns (*Dicksonia antarctica*).

[left] Bearded iris contrast in shape and texture with rounded heads of *Allium* and dainty, ruffled, pink-cream flowers of *Aquilegia*. Such planting combinations are one of the highlights at Chelsea, with seasonal splendour heralding the arrival of the forthcoming summer.

FOREWORD

Of course, it's not real. Anybody will tell you that. Gardens that appear in three weeks and then disappear overnight cannot possibly be genuine. But that does not mean they are incapable of inspiring you – spurring you on to do better. Like all gardeners, the RHS Chelsea Flower Show can make me feel inadequate, but offset against that is its capacity to fire my enthusiasm and renew my passion for gardening, which cause those few negative thoughts to fade away.

I've been coming to Chelsea every May for forty years now. There are those who become blasé about such an annual feast of floral delights, but I am not among them. For me, the RHS's Great Spring Show (to give it its proper title) is a chance to meet favourite growers, old friends and members of the gardening public who are happy to say 'hello' and chew the fat about this and that. But, above all else, it gives me a shot in the arm; it reminds me why I do the job I do, and why I was so attracted to plants and gardens in the first place.

It is no exaggeration to say that the Great Pavilion is packed with the handiwork of the world's finest growers. From the Caribbean and the Low Countries, from South Africa and Japan, all gardeners meet under the white canvas and the (hopefully) blue skies of London SW3 each year, to celebrate their skills and their passion. Only a hardened cynic could fail to be moved by their dedication and by the results of their endeavours. They will share

[below left] Chelsea is an international event, with the world's gardening media focused on it, and that includes providing daily television programmes to be broadcast.

[bottom left] A multitude of designs, materials and ideas can be created at Chelsea. Here a charity for African communities gets its message across.

[below] Nursery displays are the highlight for many visitors, with plants, such as this dazzling display of auriculas, shown off with exacting standards. Such an 'auricula theatre' could be recreated at home.

[**below right**] Many gardens are designed around a theme or central idea. In this case, an artist working in the space adds to the air of show theatre.

[**bottom right**] Each year, around 157,000 visitors come to Chelsea, which is always a favourite with the royal family. Her Majesty the Queen, here talking to HRH Prince Charles, is among the regular visitors.

[**below**] Contemporary show gardens often mix water, sculpture and planting to bold effect. To make them truly successful, precision construction is crucial.

with anyone the information and learning they have accrued over the years, and send out many green-fingered disciples to make towns and cities, villages and hamlets all over the world better places to live in.

A grandiose claim? I don't think so. Twenty-odd years of being a part of the television coverage of the RHS Chelsea Flower Show have proved to me how much people enjoy it, how much they can learn and how proprietorial they feel about this festival of flowers that erupts each year on the banks of London's River Thames.

This book is a distillation of the show's riches; a memory jogger that will last longer than the week of the show and continue to inspire you through the year. You may look

at some pictures and think 'I can't possibly do that', but there will be other gardens that will embolden you to have a go, to enrich your garden and your life with water features and wildlife ponds, pavilions and pergolas. But, above all else, without the plants and flowers everyone's lives would be the poorer and their hearts not nearly so uplifted.

You will gather from this that I rather like the RHS Chelsea Flower Show. You'd be right; and I salute a book that aims to make its fleeting glories last a little longer.

Alan Titchmarsh MBE VMH DL

Corner areas can be enlivened with dedicated seating and simple planting. Here the addition of a subterranean water feature provides an extra focal point. The result is a cool calm retreat that uses every bit of the space.
Stephen Woodhams, Barnsley House Spa Garden, 2006

INTRODUCTION

Since 1912, the Royal Horticultural Society has hosted the most prestigious flower show in the world. For six days towards the end of May, a small site (4.5 hectares/ 11 acres) in the grounds of the Royal Hospital, London, is transformed into displays of jaw-dropping horticulture. The show welcomes all types of gardeners, and is a cue for them collectively to enjoy one simple pleasure – gardening.

The RHS Chelsea Flower Show sets the tone for the years ahead: it is where horticultural ideas get aired, messages imparted and developments publicised. It gets people's minds racing, with possibilities for what you may want from your garden and gives creative answers to questions you may not have even thought about. In short, it offers something for almost every taste in gardening. The show brings together designers, nurserymen, enthusiastic amateurs and educational establishments, all of whom give their take on horticulture. Yet it is also the visitors who help make the show special. Stand in among the throng and you get to hear heartfelt honest opinions – you soon learn if a display is popular or not. Such wide-ranging diversity of opinion makes Chelsea stimulating, exciting and, for exhibitors, pretty scary.

Horticultural variety is displayed in three main elements at the show: the Great Pavilion, the show gardens and the trade stands. The pavilion hosts the splendour and spectacle of horticulture at its best: rows of flowers in ultimate bloom; planting scenes showing off a nursery's deft touch; and sublime floral displays. The show gardens are the domain of the designers, demonstrating garden-making at its best. Finally, the trade stands, dotted throughout the show ground, allow the

horticultural industry to showcase its range of products – from sit-on tractors to greenhouses.

The planning, co-ordination and energy needed to pull off any kind of display are huge. So why do people, whether amateur plant collector or renowned designer, do it? In short, it is the thrill of possibly receiving an RHS gold medal, and being able to talk with like-minded professionals and amateur gardeners. For designers, there is the added attraction of being able to work with, or predict, new planting trends; to try out ideas or materials; to help sponsors impart a message; or possibly even to attract new commissions.

[above] Once all the show gardens, nursery displays and trade stands have been perfected and judged, the RHS Chelsea Flower Show opens to the public on the Tuesday of the last week in May.

[below] At the show, visitors are able to discuss ideas or techniques with a host of exhibitors, designers and professionals. From bulb planting, flower arranging, garden design and even furniture-making, there are experts on almost all areas of garden design.

[top] In Eastern Avenue, which is attractively framed by mature London plane trees, are many of the trade stands. These may offer treats from handmade pots and garden ornaments to bespoke tree houses and safety platforms for hedge cutting.

[above] The show is a great gardening day out and is boosted by the sense of collective enjoyment and an air of 'English summer party'.

To stage a Chelsea show garden – of any size – is a considerable cost, and each designer relies on a sponsor (see panel, p13) to help in part or fully with the cost; contractors, material suppliers and associated supporters are also involved. A good Chelsea show garden should inform, inspire and suggest possibilities, and most of the 157,000 visitors normally find at least one aspect of a garden from which they can draw ideas. The small ('urban' or 'courtyard') show gardens at Chelsea are similar in size to those in a newly developed garden plot, and they measure up to 5 x 7m (16 x 22ft), while the larger ('show') ones can be up to 10 x 22m (30 x 70ft). Even though they mirror the scale of many

Chelsea garden selection... and judging

Each show garden at the RHS Chelsea Flower Show is planned at least a year in advance. The whole entry process to the show is controlled by the RHS Gardens Panel, which comprises 12 people from the RHS and gardening industry. It meets in August the year preceding a show to decide what should be seen at the following year's Chelsea. The selection process can be long and requires acute understanding of garden-making. For it, each designer submits a client's brief and drawings of the show garden, but, according to Andrew Wilson, Chair of Assessors for the RHS, 'We don't redesign gardens but we do offer comments about certain elements.' All show gardens for the following year are selected by November. From then on is a frantic time for each designer, contractor, grower and sponsor.

About three weeks before the RHS Chelsea Flower Show opens, the garden assessors receive copies of the updated client's brief. They use these as part of the judging process, to pinpoint the main points of each garden.

On the Sunday before Chelsea opens to the public, the assessors spend 20–25 minutes of detailed scrutiny on each garden. By the end of that day there is a proposed mark roughly based on: 10 points for brief and purpose of garden; 20 points for originality; 20 points for construction; 20 points for overall design; and 30 points for planting. The assessors present their mark sheet to the judges (comprising designers, contractors and growers) who then, with the assessors, look at each show garden again on the Monday. Voting takes place and a final set of marks is agreed on. 'But they are, technically, just a guide,' explained Wilson. The assessors and judges then go to 'moderation', at lunchtime on the Monday, when a balanced view of each show garden is presented by the RHS moderators. Once the medals are ratified there is no change; awards are distributed at 7am on the Tuesday.

private gardens, there is an important issue to remember. Chelsea show gardens are stage sets, created for their ability to wow and excite, in which the walls may not be made as they would be in a 'real' garden; the planting combinations may not be sustainable for long-term growth; some plants may have been forced on or kept back to ensure they flower at the end of May; and the longevity of materials chosen wouldn't survive a season in a 'normal' garden. Despite this, after Chelsea has ended, show gardens are often relocated – maybe to a school, housing association or private client.

In some ways, Chelsea feels like a show split in two. The first part involves the tension of the build-up, finishing the gardens and the judging for the medals on the Monday morning. Then, in the afternoon, the show relaxes slightly during the visit by the royal family, affording nurserymen, designers and trade representatives time to meet the royals. On the Tuesday, the awards are announced and the public throng the show until the bitter end, on the Saturday. Then everyone, tired but exhilarated, departs – with bundles of flowers in the arms of the fortunate few.

Yet, for all the pomp, ceremony, hard work and money on display, the common interest of gardening, and really wanting to make a garden better, perhaps underline why the RHS Chelsea Flower Show continues to be such an enduring success.

[above] Dramatic views and convincing design make up many Chelsea show gardens. Some such as this one give the convincing impression that they are ready for immediate use.

[right] Most designers want to establish a special atmosphere and points of interest in their private space, and this show garden has them in spades. The view through the multistemmed tree is into a lower space, suggesting further areas of interest in the garden.

[left] Every part of a Chelsea show garden must be meticulously planned, designed, built and cared for. The final tweaking continues right until the judges arrive for the last time, before casting their votes.

Matching idealism with reality

With the average cost of a Chelsea show garden being £150,000, it is essential to secure a sponsor, yet for a designer this search can be harder than designing the garden itself. He or she can spend months seeking money, or else they can sit back and hope a sponsor comes along. Sometimes the designer's idea is pitched to a potential sponsor, while at other times a designer secures a sponsor first and then works out the design.

'In an ideal world the green light from the sponsor comes in June,' said Andy Sturgeon, winner of many gold-medal show gardens at Chelsea. Once the design has been agreed, the detail of the garden gets worked up and is submitted to the RHS Gardens Panel for approval (see panel, p11). Until acceptance is received (by late autumn), designers have something of a dilemma. In the interim they have to go out and buy all the plants without even knowing if they will be awarded a plot.

From February, press releases and PR activity for RHS Chelsea Flower Show ramp up excitement levels and, according to Sturgeon, 'help put the pressure on you as the designer. As you start to visit your plants, you really get a feel for how the design might end up looking.'

The contractor starts on site in early May: trees go in during the first week, with all the construction (ideally) being finished after 12 days, leaving a week to complete the planting. However, most gardens aren't finished until Sunday afternoon – or even later, aided by van headlights. That day and the Monday can be a really stressful time for each designer, while assessing and judging are taking place.

Monday is press day, too, when each designer needs to give interviews to the media. 'That night you try to catch up on your sleep but you can't until the medals are put out on the winning gardens. This is done early on Tuesday morning, and there are always tears – either of joy or sadness,' reflected Sturgeon.

By using a curved low-level wall, an arced rod canopy and different plant types (from low-growing ferns to multistemmed shrubs), this garden feels much bigger than it actually is, and is a great inspiration for people with a small plot at home.

A City Haven' Courtyard Garden, Harpak Design, 2007

CHELSEA STYLE

Over the years the RHS Chelsea Flower Show has helped to endear us to many garden styles. From cottage gardens to formal areas, wildflower meadows to contemporary spaces, the gardens have used an array of styles, materials and ideas. Yet, increasingly, few gardens fit easily into a pigeon hole of a defined 'style', because designers have blended elements of different genres into their exhibits.

[left] An understanding of spatial division is at the heart of great contemporary design, which here has a restrained, interesting and modern feel.

[below] In their romantic gardens, Chelsea designers often include escapist elements such as this boat amid the billowing planting, to entice visitors to revel in their dreams.

Some of these mixed-style gardens are themed and relay a message, while other types of show garden might be artistic or conceptual. Either way, they may use formal or romantic elements (for example), but they can't be defined as a 'formal' or 'romantic' garden *per se*. And it is often this amalgamation of styles that makes the RHS Chelsea Flower Show so utterly absorbing, as visitors question what they see and think differently about a preconceived notion of a particular garden style.

ROMANTIC

Possibly one of the most popular garden styles seen at Chelsea, successful romantic gardens should exude masses of atmosphere, include an abundance of planting and evoke a feeling of femininity and sumptuousness. This can be a big challenge for garden designers, especially as so much depends on successful planting – roses, bearded iris, flowering shrubs and colour-coordinated summer bedding are just a few prerequisites. The end result should be an attractively planted garden, supported by a well-positioned sculpture, seating or artefact. Views should be considered so that a heightened level of enjoyment and focus can be achieved. Small areas for sitting as well as intimate spaces and hidden gems add excitement. You too can create a romantic garden relatively easily, as long as the romantic side of you is allowed unrestricted scope.

MINIMALIST

This style can often be the most divisive at Chelsea for it polarises popular opinion. Supporters respect the clean lines, the unfussy nature of the planting, the thoughtful selection of materials, the fact that such gardens can be conveniently 'low maintenance' and the consideration given to every element in such gardens. By contrast, detractors state that this contemporary style is soulless, impersonal and, because it often uses a minimal material palette, uninteresting. Whatever your take, there is no doubting the thought that designers give to create such impressive spaces. Colour can be vivid, bold and almost garish; at other times the range may be cooler, calmer and restrained. Modern contemporary gardens are particularly popular in urban environments, where gardens may not need to respond to the vernacular of local buildings and landscape as they might in the countryside. Such a style, however, isn't as easy to achieve as it looks. In really good examples, the way that people will use the space is understood, the spatial balance of the garden is exemplary, and its texture and tones of materials are well matched. If you can interpret such design principles successfully, then the end result could be hugely exciting.

MEDITERRANEAN

Simple colours, bright flowers and bold foliage, coloured rendered walls, succulent plants or cacti, outdoor furniture and shade-giving trees or screens epitomise this style. It is based on growing plants on often poor soil, with limited water, in warm dry heat. Although this is possibly the easiest garden style to conjure up in your mind – most people think of holidays past – it is actually quite difficult in

reality to achieve a convincing Mediterranean-styled garden without it looking tokenistic or inappropriate, especially if your area is prone to grey clouds and high moisture levels. Remember that terracotta is a given (whether tiled floors or containers), as is a simplicity in planting choice. But perhaps, most importantly, Mediterranean-style gardens yearn to be used and enjoyed.

ARABIC

Stone walls, coloured tiles, simplified water features, fruit trees, vertical accents of conifers or cypresses, palm trees and symbolic meanings can often be found in an Arabic garden. There is something endlessly sophisticated about the way designers interpret this style of garden at Chelsea. Restrained use of materials is important, but it is how those pieces are put together that really counts. Symmetry and geometry are essential, helping to create an air of order and gracefulness. An Arabic garden has a calm ambience that slows down the visitor and allows them fully to appreciate the scene as well as the materials and atmosphere therein. Well-conceived Arabic gardens may be difficult to create convincingly in your garden, so consider making a 'garden room' or just a part of your outdoor space based on this theme.

[above] Classically inspired schemes, here mixing contemporary detailing with formal lines, can be introduced successfully – in both large and small spaces.

[left] A bold blue wall contrasts brilliantly with the bright red of the *Bougainvillea*. Such a combination recreates a distinctly Mediterranean-type scene.

[right] The colours and textures in this restful Persian-inspired garden encourage the visitor to pause and reflect in an otherwise busy world.

CLASSIC

There is a timelessness to classic gardens that is often interpreted by other styles, fashions and people. Influences from France, English country estates and grand designs on a large-scale landscape are primary drivers. Sometimes a modern interpretation can be overlain on a classic garden, yet the tone still tends to be formal and reserved. The visitor is expected to experience a classic garden by walking through it, maybe sitting in predetermined seating areas, and having an 'arm's length' relationship with the planting. When done well, such a garden exudes an air of good quality and high class that few other garden styles can emulate. Yet these gardens are not cold or lifeless. Moreover, their structure, composition and feeling are quite easy for you to recreate in your garden.

TELLING A TALE

Chelsea designers often use their opportunity at the show to impart a message or relate a story. The end result can often be fun and good natured; at other times it can be subtle and subliminal. Some designers take their inspiration from literature or revered personalities: for example, Swedish landscape architect Ulf Nordfjell's sublime garden in 2007 paid tribute to the work of botanist, scientist and explorer Carl Linnaeus, celebrating his tercentenary and referencing the breadth of work he undertook. Others provide their interpretation of a particular topic or else recreate elements from a particular place: one garden, entitled 'I dream, I seek my garden' by Chinese garden designer Shao Fan in 2008, brought a new take on Chinese art forms, recreating a scholar's garden full of contemporary and traditional influences. Referencing an event, person or place through the medium of a show garden not only gives a firm basis for a design, but it can also be a hugely successful way of engaging with the show's visitors. In your own garden, be careful how the meaning of your story is imparted; subtlety is often safer than an overt link to a place, person or historical event, which can end up as a cliché.

WILDLIFE

Some designers use the RHS Chelsea Flower Show to emphasise the importance of wildlife in the garden and provide an understanding of how wildlife fits into the wider environment. This is often done by imparting a specific message – the reasons to garden organically or to attract certain types of wildlife, for example – or by showing that wildlife and gardening can be in harmony. Research is confirming that a balanced mix of plant types and areas of hard landscaping can offer a great habitat for wildlife. Fortunately, a diverse range of garden styles can offer attractive homes for a wide range of creatures, so overall design doesn't have to be compromised. By looking closely at the gardens on display at the show, you will

[left] A bed and a boat hint at the basis of a story, leaving the viewer to interpret the other elements of the tableau.

[below] These single flowers with their easy access for pollen are a convenient food source for the bees in this hive, while the water trough attracts a greater array of wildlife.

discover how wildlife and gardening integrate when sharing the same area. Your garden can relate to this approach, as long as it has varied garden elements and some hard landscaping.

FORMAL

There is an ingrained sense of grandeur, balance and structure in formal gardens. For a vast number of people this is fundamentally appealing, yet for others such gardens can be too rigid and unemotional. Maybe the attraction of formal gardens relates to the gardener's dominance over the natural landscape, or possibly it is because there is a natural aesthetic that balances scale and proportion, which sits comfortably with a viewer's eye. Yet again, it might be because formal rules can influence a range of other styles: modern or contemporary gardens have embraced formality; Mediterranean and Arabic gardens include formal elements; and even wildflower meadows can be created within a formal grid. You can easily introduce an element of formality into your garden, by including rounded box balls, tightly clipped hedging and restrained planting. The only challenge most gardeners face, however, is to maintain the self-discipline that is needed to keep within formal design principles.

MAGICAL AND MAD

Sometimes designers just want to throw away the shackles of tradition. Maybe they have been inspired by a painting or song, or perhaps they have had a great idea but never until RHS Chelsea Flower Show had the opportunity to build on it. Either way, these types of show gardens make for great effect.

One of the tenets is that there are no rules – the gardens are unpredictable, fun, quirky, fascinating, challenging, uncomfortable or just plain weird. Take, for example, the evocative dreaming 'girl', lying in 'The 4head garden of dreams' (designed by Marney Hall and Heather Yarrow). The living sculpture was created by Sue and Peter Hill, who used plants and other materials to create a mystical and otherworldly feel, transporting visitors into a relaxing and peaceful place. For the visiting public at Chelsea there may be confusion about the garden's intention, but sometimes that would be to miss the point: 'magical and mad' gardens celebrate diversity and are dedicated to the pursuit of creative energy. Some of these gardens may be deemed 'fun' or 'silly', but that would be to belittle the skill of making them. Trying out a style in your garden is a considerable challenge, and one that can be achieved only with the right technical skill.

[left] Arts and Crafts style gardens are often popular with show visitors because they possess a comfortable balance between scale and structure, which many people can relate to. The style is also relatively simple to recreate in your garden.

[right] Trying out new materials and different ways of using them is very much part of Chelsea's design heritage.

The long, straight lines here result from a clever use of texture and colour. Precision construction adds to the air of quality and skill. The tiered hedging, at the back of the garden, is a modern look and can be achieved with yew, box or rosemary.

The Laurent-Perrier Garden, Luciano Giubbilei, 2009

ENTRANCES, PATHS AND BOUNDARIES

At Chelsea, it really does pay to see what is happening over the garden fence.

The relationship between elements such as steps, planting, walls, furniture, water features, paving, fencing and buildings is at the heart of good design. Many of the materials used at Chelsea are available to gardeners, and designers such as Sarah Eberle (see case study, p48) and Diarmuid Gavin (see case study, p200) have worked with manufacturers on new products.

Consider first how the entrance, paving, walls, fences and steps are laid out, and what they are made of. For some, their success may lie in their use of materials that blend into the background, acting as a supporting role to plants; in other places, it may be the walls or paths that are the defining features themselves, setting the style of the garden.

Entrances can range from gates, doors and arches to trelliswork and screens. Such devices are not that often included at Chelsea, because these gardens aren't necessarily big enough to allow – or require – the space to be divided by different entrances. However, some show gardens do start off with a bold entrance (such as an archway or moon gate; see Jinny Blom case study, p46) to frame a view and really focus the attention of the visitor.

As you step into a garden, it is perhaps the material on the ground that is the next priority. From small square setts to reclaimed old York stone, from timber decking to recycled rubber mats, paving choices can be as varied as the imagination. But perhaps the main lesson from Chelsea is that the fewer materials competing for your attention the better: with paving, less really is more. This doesn't mean that having, for example, decking butting up to clay bricks laid on edge won't 'work'; it is just that thought must be given as to how these materials will look together, how they age, their construction needs and practical issues of usability. There are no rights or wrongs, but care must be paid.

Often forgotten is the role that fences or walls play. Whether it be their colours, materials or shape, how you demarcate your boundary should be given serious thought, especially when you consider just how much of a boundary you are likely to see in your day-to-day life. Walls are aesthetically appealing, but brick or stone can be hugely expensive and may need planning approval. Yet, if you are planning on staying in your house for some years, and aware that you will be seeing a lot of your boundary, then money on a wall may be well spent. The way a wall ages adds a sense of maturity to a plot and creates a microclimate of its own can never be underestimated. Fencing, too, is effective, and Chelsea designers, as ever, introduce new techniques and approaches to this type of boundary material.

2

1 **Industrial mesh** has been used as a walkway, flanked by reflective kickboards and shade-tolerant planting, resulting in a modern, clean and effective combination of materials (see case study, p102-3).

2 **Small gardens** feel bigger when boundaries are hidden from view. Ribbons of planting continue from the ground up onto the walls, as do the rounded concrete structures. Their colour, shapes and texture give little clue as to where the garden stops and starts.

3 **The relationship** of materials – 'hard' (physical entities) and 'soft' (planting) – is crucial to good design. This deck is made from Ipe timber boards set on edge, with 15mm (½in) gaps between. The gaps allow planting to soften the edges and grow between the boards.

4 **Bespoke iron** railings add interest and detail to this brick wall. With the dense hedge beyond, it is a subtle way of keeping intruders out of the garden.

1

When Chelsea designers do divide space, the end result is that a garden often feels bigger. How have they done this? Mainly by separating areas of the garden with hedging (such as box or hornbeam, often tightly clipped) or with man-made screens such as trelliswork, small walls, vertical posts, Perspex screens and glass.

One of the consistent themes running through the designs at Chelsea is that of innovation. Whether it be the designer's overall plan bringing new ideas together, or his or her collaborations with other artisans or engineers, each year sees a new or adapted technique brought to the fore. For some years, it was plastics and Perspex – whether as water sculptures, seating, tables, screens or containers. Other years have seen glass, perforated metal or rusting steel used to great effect. Recycled CDs, crushed glass mulch, recycled plastics or by-products of the timber industry have also been adopted, for planters, paths, walls or surface decoration.

The end result has been radical uses and new applications of materials, making the show gardens exciting and challenging. At Chelsea, it really does pay to see what is happening over the garden fence.

Steps with visual interest

Dealing with differences in height is a challenge – whether it be a few centimetres over a small distance or gradient changes that require substantial earth moving. The principle for either is the same, though. The gardener is required to move soil or rock into level areas so that access is made bearable by users of that space.

While steps are a practical and physical necessity for most, they also add much in terms of visual interest; in addition, their design contribution should not be underestimated. From contemporary clean lines to rustic charm, from recycled to manufactured materials, steps can be created from an almost endless list of possibilities. Technical concerns, such as structural rigidity and comfort of travel, must also be considered, as well as the safety of steps, especially taking into account how different materials respond in different weather conditions.

EXPERT TIP

Adam Frost
How to design your steps

❛ Altering levels in a garden adds interest and movement and is often necessary. Such a change can be enhanced by using steps that are more generously sized than maybe they need to be in order to make an area look wider than it actually is. This works well when approaching a door or gate. At the other end of the spectrum, keeping steps shallow and narrow can add to a sense of tension when entering a space.

Key points to think about when you are creating steps:

- When choosing the materials for your steps, take your lead from the other surfaces in the garden. Timber steps tend to be an easy and cheap way of dealing with level changes, while steps made from hard materials will require concrete foundations. Also bear safety in mind, especially for your choice of tread material (the actual step itself). Non-slip materials may be appropriate in some circumstances.
- A visual warning of the change in level is needed, possibly by laying a different material at the top of the flight.
- People should be able to travel up and down steps comfortably. To achieve this, the general rule is to have

STEPPING UP TO THE MARK

Steps can be simple or complicated, made in a range of design styles, for short- or long-term use.

1 Log cuts have been set on end to give a rustic and 'eco' feel to this subtly sweeping stepped path. The use of varying size, length and girth adds interest, but can give a relatively uneven walking surface.

2 Beige-white diamond-sawn limestone slabs give a clean contemporary feel, accentuated by the dark shadows underneath. The soft grasses and other perennials reinforce the linear nature of the stone.

3 Clever effects have been achieved with a variety of materials. The mesh-topped gabions (filled with rock) give an industrial feel and contrast with the more 'domestic', smooth walls and cobbled pathway.

4 When small changes in level are required, an obvious difference in material can help prevent the step becoming an unnecessary hazard. The interplay between the colour and textural difference of the two materials also makes for interest.

the rise of the step around 15cm (6in) high and the tread should never be smaller than 30cm (12in) across.

- Steps need to be inviting, and wider flights can be more welcoming than narrow ones.
- Changes of direction such as a curve or sweep in the flight of steps gives the user several vistas onto the garden as they proceed up or down.
- Lit steps can look beautiful and add an enchanting air of elegance, as well as safety at night-time.
- For a steep flight of steps, it may be necessary to create a grab rail (this could either a freestanding or wall mounted design) for people to use as a support. *"*

Achieving the correct rise and tread is crucial to ensure a flight of steps is comfortable and user-friendly.

Walls for vertical wonder

At first sight, the physical presence of a wall might seem an immovable oppressive feature. Yet, with imagination and a clear understanding of your plot, a wall can offer an array of possibilities: it can be painted or faced to change its colour or texture; it can be planted against or on, bringing vegetation to a vertical plane; it can act as a microclimate allowing for a wide range of plants to be grown; and it could be created into something sculptural and visually exciting. Practical concerns, of course, must be thought through. What direction is the wall facing? Will it be mainly sunny or shaded? How high is it? Is there any planting area at its base? Who owns the structure? Will any changes affect the rigidity of it? But once these serious questions are answered, a wall need not be a blight on the gardener's landscape – with creativity and flair it could become a great gardening asset.

SMOOTH WALLS AND CLEAN FINISHES

With a little bit of imagination and some appropriate design, walls can be transformed into stylish and contemporary features.

1 By dividing the face of this large wall into sections filled with climbing ivy (*Hedera*), this living backdrop exudes permanence and solidity.

2 Rammed earth walls display a stunning patina of colour and pattern. The textured finish is a great backdrop to the planting in front.

3 Moss tracks have been inset into a smooth finish render, but this example would need irrigation to prevent the moss drying out on a vertical structure. Moss must never be collected from wild areas.

FORM AND TEXTURE

Walls can have three dimensions and be full of pace, movement and creativity.

1 A row of painted and natural, stripped-bark trunks forms a 'moving' wall. Because of this bold design statement, the surrounding planting needs to complement not compete with the wall.

2 Stacked Crosland Hill sandstone slabs, laid completely dry, are a sublime take on a modern dry-stone wall.

3 Rusting steelwork, cut and carved into a chequerboard shape, not only conceals the far wall but also makes a huge statement. This structure houses birch (*Betula*) trees behind it – the white-grey of the trunks can be glimpsed through the open squares. Over time, the steel will darken.

The size of this garden has been accentuated by use of strong horizontals (white-painted walls) and verticals (white bark on the birch trees). This technique, coupled with overflowing planting, helps reduce the dominance of paths and walls.

The Savills Garden, Marcus Barnett and Philip Nixon, 2006

LOW-KEY FENCING

Fences are most commonly made of wood or metal. Their role can be subtle or obvious, and should always reflect the surrounding aesthetic.

1 Reused pieces of timber have been nailed together to create an informal but highly successful spatial divide, allowing roses to grow and entwine through them.

2 Hooped-ring iron railings may have a municipal feel to them, but here have been 'softened' by the stunning display of red poppies and other wild flowers. The formality of the railings makes for an interesting contrast with the informality of the annual flowers.

3 In urban areas, especially in terraced housing, front garden spaces play a significant role in 'greening' the urban environment. Here, contemporary tapered-end, wooden posts show where public space ends and private garden begins. The gaps between each post 'soften' the look of the fencing and allow plants to grow through them.

Defining space: fences and screens

Whether it is your boundary or an internal area, how you divide up a garden is an essential part of design. The use of fencing for such divisions is a feature for many outdoor plots, and there are a range of sizes, colours and materials to select. Their style, strength and longevity need consideration, whether it be of formal, traditional iron railings or more informal, rustic wooden examples. Practical concerns of how the fence is secured into the ground are also important, as are whether the fence abuts a public space and what could grow on or against it.

Screens, on the other hand, tend to subdivide space within an existing garden area – to create pockets of interest, provide backdrops and focal points, or to suggest direction of travel. Their role and creation must be well thought through – it is never easy to move a physical structure.

STYLISH SCREENS FOR PERSONAL SPACE

Screens – whether large or small, man-made or natural, coloured or textured – can actually help make a garden feel bigger.

1 Orange, smooth-rendered walls create a dramatic backdrop. The subtle curve to the screen matches the sculptural boulders in the foreground, while the colour links to some of the flowers.

2 This white screen not only curves round a corner but also folds over at the top a little, triggering a sense of enclosure and safety for those sitting on the glass deck below.

3 Toughened glass is increasingly used in gardens to divide space while permitting light and views through.

Stylish and useful paths

How you traverse your space and how it looks are fundamental factors in creating paths or walking surfaces through a garden. Paths can meander at a gentle pace, encouraging you to absorb the surroundings, or they can aid quick and easy movement to a specific area. Decisions should focus on: what the role of the path is to be; how long it is expected to last; what level of maintenance is required; and what types of materials could be used. Consider also the physical presence of the path, and how its inclusion may divide or harmonise your space. If your garden includes a dominant path as a central design feature, then its materials and construction must be of a very high quality – it will come under scrutiny from all quarters. Natural stone is a popular choice of path material, while other hard landscaping materials can sometimes provide much needed colour.

1

MATERIAL INTEREST

Curving paths are popular in less formal design schemes, softening the overall route through a garden.

1 This raised and curved walkway consists of wooden decking and circular concrete 'landing pads'.

2 Wet pointing has been used to keep the path's stone in place. Note how the edging of the path follows the shape of the stone itself, adding a quasi-natural feel to the overall effect.

3 The rough nature of these bricks adds a texture and colour variation to the path. By including such a path in a home scheme, visual interest is maintained throughout the year, as well as providing a complementary backdrop to the planting.

2

3

GETTING STRAIGHT TO THE POINT

Simple linear paving is often attributed to modern designs, but can be used for any style garden. The result is often a pared-down approach, allowing the materials themselves or associated planting to shine.

1 Diamond-sawn sandstone slabs divide the water's edge from the planting. The buff-beige colour acts as a cool and subtle tone; the fact that the slabs have been precision cut adds a contemporary feel.

2 This long view through dense, low-growing planting shows how well a path can be confined to a supporting role. By allowing the plants to overspill the edges, an informal effect is created and the visitor is encouraged to carry on and reach the end of the path.

3 A cuboid theme linking the wood block seat and square stone blocks beneath is complemented by use of the same stone for the longer slabs flanking the water feature. This design principle brings consistency and uniformity to the space.

4 A shaped path adds interest and visual stimulation to a garden. Here, warm-coloured, Flemish brick paving setts attractively offset the dense, pretty planting, which includes a white peony (see case study, p78).

Curves abound aplenty in this garden, taking the eye from the ageing gnarled olive tree and the low wooden dividing walls across to the timber boardwalk and beyond. The vertical 'water wall' also helps take the eye away from the perimeter and focus interest into the internal space.

The Lloyds TSB Garden, Trevor Tooth, 2008

EXPERT TIP

Adam Frost
Rammed earth walls

' Though it has seen a revival in recent years, this method of walling construction is an ancient one – the materials having been available to humans longer than any other. Added to that is the fact that they are naturally available, which gives the walls very good green credentials, so why not try creating one in your garden. Typically, a rammed earth wall is 30–35cm (12–14in) thick. It can be constructed using form work (usually timber), which is set up to create the desired shape. Make the walls from a damp material (mixed soil, water and lime), filled on average 20cm (8in) at a time and then compacted with a power tamper. Repeat this process until the wall has reached the desired height. At this point, remove the form work and seal the wall to prevent water penetrating the materials. '

Rammed earth walls can make a dramatic backdrop within a garden as well as demonstrating an unusual use of materials.

TAKE ON TRADITION

Many gardeners will use slabs or bricks for a pathway or patio, but the material chosen should be similar to, or at least complementary to, the adjacent architecture.

1 Grey setts have been used as both paving material and for the raised wall. Some of the gaps have been filled by self-sown plants.

2 The bricks here have been laid in a basket-weave formation. Their colour variation adds interest and gives a randomness to the otherwise orderly paving approach.

3 This garden offers plenty of real-life suggestions for improving an outside space. The random concrete paving is similar to that found in most garden centres or DIY shops, and it sits well with the raised pond, mixed planting and table and chair.

4 Main paths lead off from a circular passing space, with bricks laid in a running bond, but in different directions. The result is a considered, well-executed and interesting design.

Making that important entrance

How you physically enter – or indeed view – a garden can set the ambience and anticipation level for your enjoyment, so the composition is all important. A hidden glimpse over a wall or through a fence can engender an expectation of surprise or adventure, while a formal, defined and focused approach may set a predetermined tone to the space. Entrances don't always have to be obvious, however; sometimes, the more subtle examples can prove just as effective. For many gardens, though, the reality is that a garden is entered through a back door, side gate or patio doors, where views may be harder to frame or create. Because of this, thought must always be given to a sense of arrival and what design techniques could be used to enhance or augment such transitions; and what you should feel or experience as you go through the gate or door.

LOW-KEY WELCOME

Defining private space not only establishes limits but can also set the tone for the space beyond.

1 A rustic fence ties in well with the stepping stones, cobble infill and random planting beyond. All the elements (building, hard landscaping and planting) of this design work as a unified whole.

2 Ironwork railings have a traditional feel, and plants have been allowed to soften the overall effect. Designed for a banker, the shapes represent percentage symbols, proving that humour can be incorporated into any scheme.

COME ON IN

That all-important first view into a garden can be vital to the overall enjoyment of an outside area, so from the outset consider how people will physically enter your space.

1 This structured and well-proportioned garden uses a suite of traditional Swedish materials in a pared-down but considered way. A sense of 'what next?' is created by the path being staggered, and at the far end white-flowering foxgloves beckon the visitor still further.

2 Undulating mounds of moss frame the view into this garden, hinting at a private room beyond. Beware, however: the moss would soon dry out and it would be near impossible to keep it looking like this. Moss is a rare material in gardens and should only ever be used if guaranteed to have come from a sustainable, legitimate source.

3 The bold, Chinese-inspired moon gate entrance may be visible, but its path through is somewhat hidden by the arrangement of hard and soft materials in the foreground. Full of symbolism and meaning, the passage through the circular entrance leads to another defined area.

LAURENT-PERRIER GARDEN

Many gardens at Chelsea are based on a theme – whether that be pictoral, interpretative or cerebral. The successful ones, however, work best when they are appreciated by people who may or may not know the theme – and here, Jinny Blom succeeded on both levels. This garden was not only pretty, but also well structured, balanced and meaningful. It used masses of 'soft' planting to unify the space, while including three circular shapes which together created a moon gate. This formal sculptural element was balanced beautifully by the plants and associated paving. The result was a calm, tranquil and genuine example of what you could do with a private garden of 10 x 23m (33 x 70ft) in size.

It is true to say that many, if not most, successful garden designers are influenced by other masters of their art. In this instance, the designer created a garden that paid homage to the 1950s Italian architect Carlo Scarpa. In plan, it had different areas of hard landscaping 'pads' countered by dense planting beds; the different number of routes through the garden at varying levels represented 'a journey through the shifting and unpredictable moments in life'. This may sound a little grand, but the reality was pretty close. If you wanted to search it out, the symbolism of life's journey, of beginning at the front of the space in youth and ending at the back of the garden in old age, could easily be 'read'. But if not, then the planting on its own carried you along, giving visual consistency across the space.

CONSIDER ALSO SOME OF THE KEY DESIGN ELEMENTS:

- the three circular shapes (at the entrance a transparent bronze solar gate, near the middle a 'floating' lunar gate and at the back a red sandstone disc) give structure and focus throughout the garden;
- when viewed on their own, they are circular sculptures, but when observed head on (as in this photograph) they merge to create a moon gate;
- planting is very strong, with a mix of grasses and herbaceous perennials mingling to give a 'floating' atmosphere – no soil can be seen;
- edges of steps or paths appear to be invisible because of the plants around;
- the fastigiate (columnar) oaks, which play sentry to the irregular path, and dense hornbeam hedge (along the boundary) give a green backdrop to the oranges, blues, whites and pinks of the flowers;
- a rectangular, low-level, flat water feature (at the back) gives a different, more open and reflective atmosphere – perhaps symbolising maturity and age as the visitor edges ever nearer the final red sandstone disc.

1 A circular sculpture, the first of three, sets the tone for this garden. Here, the transparent bronze 'solar' gate symbolises life beginning, and it balances perfectly with the two sculptures beyond. A strong focal point can be created in any garden, and it helps the viewer orientate him- or herself throughout the space.

DESIGNER Jinny Blom

CONTRACTOR Crocus.co.uk

AWARD Gold

CATEGORY Show Garden, 2007

SPONSOR Laurent-Perrier (UK) Ltd

KEY WORDS flowery; 'floating'; informal; moon gates; focal point; relaxing

IN A SENTENCE... A clever garden that uses the concept of moon gates to give vertical structure, while the underplanting is informal and endlessly pretty.

2 Colours and textures in an endless range cover the whole space, unifying it and giving it lots of interest. In this really strong, well-planted garden, the grasses include *Stipa gigantea* and *S. tenuissima*, and the flower colour comes from orange bearded iris and *Geranium sylvaticum* 'Mayflower'.

3 Two separated circular sculptures maintain the focal point in this space: one, a 'lunar' gate suspended above a pond; the other, a solid circular sandstone disc.

4 Columnar oak trees, specifically used for tall 'accent' planting, give a subtle vertical scale; note that they also help balance the three circular sculptures. Vertical height helps trick the eye into thinking the space is bigger than it actually is, by taking the eye away from the ground plan.

5 The paved areas are set at differing 90-degree intervals, and at differing heights. Symbolically they signify the challenging transitions in life, but in reality they bring colour and practicality to the space. They make the movement down the garden more surprising and tonally link with the moon gate.

6 A tall hornbeam hedge around the boundary helps offset the planting, paving and sculptures. Its dense green allows the flower colours to be seen and helps 'frame' the whole composition.

WALKING BAREFOOT WITH BRADSTONE

Sometimes with Chelsea there can be a tendency to remember the really extrovert gardens, the ones that got all the television and newspaper coverage. Often they used an iconic image or were so startling for their visual trickery that they drilled a hole into your brain. But then there were other, equally successful gardens like this. Seeing it in 2006, many visitors were bowled over by its calmness, the simplicity of it. It worked, because it used a reduced set of colours and tones, and because it stuck to a consistent design element – here, it was curves. The design had self-confidence, ability and quality oozing through it, many attributes that gardeners would sincerely like to emulate.

Garden designer Sarah Eberle was, until Chelsea 2006, probably best known for her blockbuster show gardens at the sister RHS Flower Show at Hampton Court Palace (which takes place in early July). However, for Chelsea, she wanted to create a simpler garden, one that was 'a sensual delight, with elements to see, listen to, smell and touch'. Added to this was a desire to make the garden more environmentally conscious, so she used paving manufacturer Bradstone's water drainage system, which collected then reused water from around the garden for irrigation and the ornamental pool. The result was inspiring.

THE DESIGNER HAS USED:

- a range of hard landscaping textures: the circular paving setts, a smooth rendered bench and a concrete column wall;
- dense green planting and splashes of white flowers, which give consistency to the overall space, even though the amount of planting is quite limited;
- a shallow water pool, which occupies a large amount of the garden but to great effect; it is quite shallow, but the water shows reflections and provides a sense of movement;
- abundant curves, from the dining area, paving and planting through to the small open garden room in the far corner;
- an element of surprise: the water level rises and falls, sometimes flooding the causeway linking the paved area to the garden room (not shown in the photograph)... but there is just enough depth for people to feel as if they are 'walking on water'.

1 Curves have been used to give a consistent approach, which is a feature of all good design. The rendered retaining wall has two purposes: it not only holds back the dense planting behind, but it also gives the visitor some soft curves to lead the eye from one area to another. In addition, its smoothness helps give a simple texture to the space.

DESIGNER Sarah Eberle in conjunction with Andrew Herring

CONTRACTOR Hillier Landscapes

AWARD Gold

CATEGORY Show Garden, 2006

SPONSOR Bradstone

KEY WORDS muted palette; calm; simple; textures; curves; water; grey

IN A SENTENCE... An often under-rated garden that has a great sense of peace and tranquillity to it, supported by lovely design touches.

2 Different sized, rounded setts are used as paving, and they continue the curved theme. Their grey/buff colour can look sombre in some locations, but notice how the planting 'lifts' them, backed by the darker water and lighter retaining and boundary walls.

3 A lower curved path allows visitors to access the small garden room at the end (to the far right, but not seen here). But beware: the water level is constantly rising and falling, so sometimes visitors can walk along in the dry; at other times their feet will get wet. The reflection of the wall in the water created a tremendous focus and stillness.

4 *In situ* **concrete columns**, topped by a deep horizontal concrete coping, bring a vertical harmony to the garden by using similar colours and shapes to those in the ground plan and on retaining walls. What goes on along a garden's boundary is often as important as what goes into it, and this can be easily forgotten in home gardens.

5 Dense planting has been used to offset the greys and muted tones of the water and the hard landscaping. The consistent repetition of white flowers and dark green foliage is intentional – the designer wanted to ensure that the mass of green really did offset the hard landscaping colour and textures.

PLANTING

The plants really are the stars
in any garden and at Chelsea
this is definitely the case:
they provide the colour, drama
and excitement that engages
gardeners at all levels.

For many people, Chelsea is about the plants and, as Chelsea is a flower show, it would be unimaginable for flowers not to take pride of place. Whether rare or unusual, in the Great Pavilion or show gardens, they often 'make' the gardens. From modernist designs using lines of hedges to cottage-garden combinations crowded with irises or roses, Chelsea's displays satisfy the need to be inspired.

The RHS Chelsea Flower Show sets the tone for the gardening year. It feels like the start of the season, even though most people will already have started growing seed and establishing plants. Being confronted by the colour and combinations of the plants on display makes you yearn for the summer ahead.

Yet, among this exuberance it is worth having a reality check. Not every type of plant can be shown in late spring – those that flower in autumn or winter can't be fooled into thinking May is their natural flowering time. And, in addition, not everything at Chelsea is as nature intends. Some dazzling combinations are artificially contrived,

and certain plants would never grow together in the open ground; correct planting distances are usually ignored so as to stage a stronger display; and what is on show is often protected from the vagaries of weather. These factors shouldn't undermine the displays, but they are best viewed with open eyes.

So, what can be seen? Cottage-garden abundance with endless colour; swathes of prairie-style planting; crisp lines of contemporary combinations; and trees and shrubs that give structure and maturity. This list could go on for pages, but essentially Chelsea's planting can be experienced in three broad categories: the Pavilion's floral displays; planting 'scenes' within the Pavilion; and the show gardens. The floral displays are an opportunity to see horticulture at its best and individual plants at their peak. From roses to lilies, sweet peas to *Verbascum*, the showmanship is exceptional. The same is true of the Pavilion's 'scenes', where exhibitors show combinations of plants and suggest how these plants could be grown outside. And finally, there are the show gardens which use plants to create an inspiring effect, often for visual drama or to impart a meaning (such as ideas for shady corners). These gardens can include trees or aquatic plants, shrubs or meadows, perennials or vegetables.

One of the most fascinating aspects of Chelsea is the way growers coax plants to perform, especially when displaying in The Great Pavilion. From daffodils that have been kept in cold storage to delay bud-burst to

1 Trees provide maturity and structure in show gardens, as well as a sense of scale.

2 Mixing colours and textures is crucial for visual interest. Here, evergreen *Viburnum rhytidophyllum* is the backdrop to silver-leaved *Stachys byzantina*, rounded balls of *Allium* and purple spires of *Salvia*, which combine to strong effect.

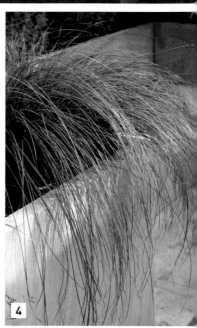

the rain. There are hundreds of such tricks. So what does all this passion and skill produce? Many people talk of plant trends coming from Chelsea. In some years, a certain colour such as purple or green might dominate; in other years, there is a reliance on texture or leaf shape. Often plants such as *Allium*, bearded iris, *Aquilega* or umbellifers will steal the show. Alternatively it may be a dazzling display of dahlias (shown for the first time in 2009) that take the breath away. Naturally inspired planting combinations have really come to the fore in recent years, blending plants to lead the visitor's view through and across the space; purple *Allium* flowers, nodding *Stipa gigantea* grass and spires of herbaceous perennials are now popular design techniques.

Planting can also reflect the mood of society or follow fashion: Tom Stuart-Smith's garden in 2008 (see case study, p78) led the way in muted tones, perhaps reflecting social uncertainty in the economy at that time. New techniques include green roofs, vertical planting on walls and ornamental meadows. Whether you are a new gardener or experienced visitor, the display of plants at Chelsea will give you an opportunity to stop and indulge in this melting pot of horticultural splendour, blended with a large dose of showmanship. Who could ask for more?

summer-flowering dahlias that have been forced to flower early, both require great skill. This isn't just about manipulating growing conditions; it requires planning and precision to ensure the growing requirements over the annual life cycle of that plant are mimicked. Some last-minute techniques are often required: for example, hair dryers are used to open up a flower bud and foam coffee cups can be placed over flowers to protect them from

3 This clean contemporary design uses just one genus – a succulent, *Sempervivum* – and relies on the interplay between plant form and container style to provide interest.

4 The long thin leaves of this grass soften the edge to this raised bed and are seemingly back-lit by the creamy white stone behind.

A modern tale

When describing design, many commentators and designers use the word 'modern' to reflect a contemporary style that, in essence, is about an apparent simpleness in planting combinations: maybe a few species of plants have been used, or the same plant repeated within a space. However, the visual result can often belie the intricate nature of the planting and the complexity of selecting the plants. Appropriate plant choice is essential for a scheme if it is to hold together, especially if more contemporary hard materials, sculpture or furniture are to be used. Consider planting in blocks or swathes, and remember that foliage and texture are as important as flower colour and seasonal variation. With a little planning, modern planting design can be a year-round addition to any garden.

COMBINING OLD AND NEW

Although mixing different plants together is nothing new, bringing a contemporary touch to the scheme can create plantings that are timely and interesting.

1 Blocks of plants have been expertly put together, with a simple palette of green foliage and white flowers. In the foreground white *Iris* merge with the taller spires of white *Digitalis*, while white *Viburnum opulus* 'Roseum' flourishes below the birch trees.

2 Silvery, sword-like leaves of *Astelia chathamica* contrast with the burgundy dwarf bearded *Iris* in front in this modern planting scheme, where flowering and foliage plants have been intermingled.

3 Modernist-inspired planting elements work well together in this garden. They are the formal clipped box hedge, the billowing and frothy planting within, the wispy wands of grass *Stipa gigantea* nodding in the air and the raised canopy of the tree beyond.

ARCHITECTURAL TAKE

Putting plants with distinctive foliage or flowers together can create a bold impression.

1 These three different plants (pink-red flowering *Cirsium rivulare* 'Atropurpureum', tropical-looking *Canna* and variegated grass *Phalaris arundinacea*) work well together in a Chelsea show garden, but they wouldn't do so when planted this closely in a real garden.

2 Rounded box (*Buxus*) balls are very popular with designers for their consistent colour and shape. Here the spheres combine with grasses and other clipped shrubs for contrasting effect.

The enduring appeal of cottage gardens

Ask most first-time, and in fact many seasoned, gardeners what their favourite style of planting is and it will probably be cottage gardens. For many decades, the appeal of plants growing together in an apparently random manner has touched the sentimental bone in most observers. There is something informal, uncontrived and undesigned about this style of planting. Yet cottage gardens require quite a lot of maintenance to ensure a

balance is achieved, as well as an understanding of how plants grow – and compete – together to have a hope of succeeding for the long term. Chelsea gardens demonstrate that this style is for the romantic in each and every one of us, allowing all to forget about colour rules or textural definition; instead, cottage garden planting encourages you to sit back and enjoy the variety and display that so often is on offer in many gardens.

CELEBRATION IN DIVERSITY

Mixing plant shapes, colours and habits is at the core of this seemingly informal but planterly style.

1 Creamy yellow summer bedding plants, which help give that hit of summer colour, mix well with the rounded leaves of *Alchemilla mollis*, the silvery grey *Artemisia* and the burgundy-red sweet Williams.

2 Even though there is a faintly contemporary feel to this garden's stone walls, the planting is decidedly informal and cottagey.

3 This quiet detail of planting along a path typifies cottage gardens, with their clumps of purple-blue *Nepeta* and *Alchemilla mollis* growing under pink sun roses (*Cistus*).

4 In this modern take on rural French planting, bearded *Iris* has been primarily used at the front of the planting area. The box (*Buxus*) balances with the wall beyond, and helps anchor the *Iris* in between.

5 The dominant reds of corn poppy (*Papaver rhoeas*) bring this scene alive, while the white-flowering umbellifer (purple-leaved cow parsley, *Anthriscus sylvestris* 'Ravenswing') is a useful colour addition.

6 Although this rustic scene is somewhat stage set, the wooden water butt, old-fashioned watering can and flowering lavender below conjure up a charming image.

Planting for drought

How the climate changes is of substantial importance to gardeners. Whether on a seasonal level – if one summer is hotter and drier than the previous one – or on a more long-term prediction of substantial climate change, some plantings may have to be altered over the coming years. This means that if location and aspect demand it, gardeners have to respond by selecting plants that suit and thrive in the new circumstances in that area; such changes, however, don't mean that everyone will be living in Mediterranean-style gardens next year. But, if change is required, then what a choice you are faced with – thousands of plants from all over the world are now available to gardeners, with the internet assisting seed swapping as well as the constant exchange of information and learning. Thus, as the climate changes, you can learn from others, and vice versa. Chelsea designers, too, ever keen to include new or more unusual plants, offer a raft of suitable ideas to take back to your own garden.

BOLD FORM AND STRUCTURE

Plants with silvery grey leaves, or fleshy succulent foliage, are well adapted to growing in reduced rainfall areas.

1 Bold, dark green leaves of *Cycas revoluta* make a great backdrop to this light-blue selection of summer-flowering *Agapanthus*. The background palms add to a quasi-tropical and Mediterranean feel.

2 The silvery white, hairy leaves of *Verbascum* create an eye-catching visual statement. Later in the season the yellow flower spike of the *Verbascum* may extend upwards of 1m (3ft).

3 This shallow bowl has been planted with low-growing, drought-tolerant *Sempervivum* and *Echeveria* species, mulched on top with stones (to help keep available moisture in the soil). Note how the spiky, purple-leaved *Cordyline* behind continues the colour theme.

4 Sedum matting, which is often used for creating green roofs (see p169), here welcomes random plantings of silvery blue and burgundy *Sempervivum*.

5 Although tender ***Agave americana*** 'Mediopicta Alba' will not survive outside during winters in cool-temperate regions, it does provide a stunning display in summer, given good drainage. Watch out for the spines, however, which can be very painful.

1

1

Formality and grandeur

Something about formal planting schemes transcends fashions and time. There is a consistency to their use and application in a garden that cleverly allows formal-style planting to be interpreted from historical recreation all the way through to contemporary style. And it is this ability to morph into the required overall design that makes formal plantings so popular in Chelsea show gardens. In essence, such a style includes clipped box, rows of trees, 'seas' of green and repetition of form or colour. The beauty of the planting is its simpleness, supported by the apparent control humans have over the land; there is little room or time for impromptu planting here. Such formal gardens may leave some people with a feeling that the garden is bland and regimented; but for many others it is a stylish way to design a garden – whether at Chelsea or at home.

ALL SHAPES AND SIZES

Plant selection is crucial to ensure that a formal planting scheme can be created – and maintained – in the appropriate style.

1 This substantial garden uses a range of formal techniques to sublime effect. The large blocks of box (*Buxus*) echo the linearity of the paving, while the trees give the space a cool feel; they also add height and make the area feel much bigger than it actually is. The trees are *Schinus molle*, which are subtropical and therefore not hardy in cool-temperate areas, and more hardy *Trachycarpus fortunei* palms.

2 White trunks of birch establish a feeling of a mini copse, and visually link into the white walls and white garden building at the rear. Low-growing *Rodgersia* produces a blanket of green leaves, enhanced by creamy white flowers atop.

3 *Pinus sylvestris* **'Watereri'** brings an unusual texture and colour to this garden and introduces a low hummocky feel to the area, especially when it is this tightly pruned. It is an unusual, yet totally successful planting choice.

4 Full on formality reigns here. The form of this standard pruned juniper – an unusual selection for a container – is repeated by neighbouring, tightly clipped specimens. Beware though: sometimes, too much of the same shape can be a little too repetitive, especially in a restricted space. The juniper is surrounded by *Soleirolia soleirolii*.

Colour themed

When talking to gardeners about the main role they need planting to achieve in their garden, the most common response is that it should provide some colour, whether it be clashing hues that slide and collide, or a restrained palette of just one colour consistently used. Although foliage and flower colours are a deeply personal choice, the prevailing fashion suggests that these should be harmonious rather than contradictory. Whatever the range of colours being chosen, they should work together and not end up causing a visual headache. This doesn't mean that all schemes should include soft pastels and shades – far from it. Bold and brash are often seen at Chelsea, but even then they are introduced with consideration. Colour can be added in myriad ways, whether via flower colour throughout a season or by changing foliage tones over a year. The show gardens display a snapshot of colour ideas, and it is up to individual gardeners to experiment with their own take at home.

FULL-ON COLOUR FOR FULL-ON EFFECT

Whether foliage or flower power, plants must be considered for the colour contribution they offer.

1 Blending soft colours together can give a relaxed and feminine feeling to a garden: for example, red-flowering *Geum* mixes well with lime-green and yellow *Alchemilla mollis*.

2 Yellow dominates in this informal planting combination of moisture-loving plants. These include yellow-flowering *Zantedeschia*, the curly leaves of a sedge behind and the orange-yellow flowers of *Geum*. The result is a neat little planted area.

3 Colour shapes can be created in any garden by using plants in an eye-catching and massed way. Here the designers have balanced rectangles of lawn turf with slabs of red-leaved *Heuchera* 'Peach Flambé'. In winter, the heuchera will die down so the effect would be significantly reduced.

4 A range of colours – from lavender-blue and silver through to pink-mauve, and then pink-mauve and purples – have been brought together in this clever planting and hard material scheme. The *Yucca rostrata*, in the centre, with its dramatic spherical head of fine blue leaves, can tolerate a little frost.

EXPERT TIP

Tom Stuart-Smith
Layered planting

❝ The idea behind layered planting in the garden is to repeat the ecological patterns inherent in complex plant communities. In an oak woodland, for example, there are various different levels: an upper canopy; often a middle canopy of medium-sized trees and saplings; a shrub layer; a herb layer; and then bulbs and corms at the bottom. By adapting this natural pattern to a garden, it is possible to have different layers flowering at different times, usually with the lower layers flowering first. ❞

Using a range of plant types, such as bulbs, perennials, grasses and shrubs, builds up layers of interest and gives structure to your planting.

Colour, form and texture are at the heart of this good design. Remember that some of these planting combinations would not survive long term in a garden, and that planting density is often massively increased for great visual effect.
The Bupa Garden, Cleve West, 2008

Simplicity in minimalism

In a way, minimal planting is similar to formal planting schemes. A considered and ordered view of how to use growing material is required where each subject must warrant its inclusion based on leaf shape, overall habit, flower colour or year-round appearance. In addition, the planting must be in tune with the overall design theme, maybe referencing or supporting a colour, texture or implied meaning. What may look stunning and at the peak of growth at Chelsea, however, can be quite different in the home garden. Minimalism demands an order and exactitude of plant choice that many gardeners may find limiting, because of their desire to have a diversity in plant selection as well as year-round interest. Fortunately, in the appropriate place, and with the right planting, the style can be a sublime addition to any garden space.

ONE OF A KIND

Using just a single species of plant is frequently a great way to undertake a minimal design.

1 Low-growing mounds of *Festuca gautieri* seem to cut through the granite wedges either side of this bed and give the impression of a naturally occurring rock and plant community.

CLEAN AND SIMPLE

Careful plant selection is crucial to the success of minimalistic planting schemes.

1 The billowing and ever-changing shapes of grass *Stipa tenuissima* contrast well against the tightly clipped form of the box (*Buxus*) balls behind.

2 Young, silvery grey leaves of *Verbascum* are beautifully offset by the white-flowering, scented biennial stock (*Matthiola incana*) behind. Note how this duo also complements the silvery grey of the granite boulder in the foreground. The *Verbascum* has been planted densely here for show-stopping effect but not for long-term, sustainable plant growth.

3 Massed plantings of one plant type are often seen at Chelsea. This close-up view of bearded iris shows off the flower and leaf shape in great detail.

Planting with wildlife in mind

Although it is clear that the plants selected for any garden should be chosen as a response to the owner's wishes, the role that plant selection can have on wildlife should also be considered. A good range of plants – whether grown for foliage (such as conifers) or for flowers (such as summer bedding) – is best for a balanced sustainable garden that welcomes, and is home to, a broad range of wildlife. Current research is now finding that wildlife needs a diverse range of plant type (bulbs, annuals, herbaceous perennials, shrubs, evergreens, long grass, trees and so on); in addition, many animals and insects don't seem to worry whether plants are native or non-native. Gardeners, therefore, are in a unique position to help attract wildlife to their space, no matter where it is situated. Whether your garden is extensive or minute, wildlife and planting must go hand in hand.

SOMETHING FOR ALL

Planting with wildlife in mind should lead to a greater understanding of the potential gardeners can bring to increasing biodiversity.

1 A range of living and inanimate objects occupies this 'living tower'. The succulent plants are able to withstand limited root depth and reduced amounts of irrigation, while the old sticks and twigs offer a place for creatures. The combination is a decorative, unusual but highly effective home for wildlife.

2 A field of green wheat gives the impression of an agrarian landscape and imparts a strong message of rural stewardship and organic crop production. A show garden such as this demonstrates that planting at Chelsea concerns more than just the role of ornamental plants.

3 Annual corn poppies have seemingly self-sown in the loose gravel and stones next to the path. Such a combination of simple open flowers and informal path can prove a haven for wildlife.

4 This standard vine has been underplanted with an array of annual wild flowers, including annual chrysanthemums, typical of California meadow planting. The colour is spectacular and a significant addition to any garden.

3

4

EXPERT TIP
Nigel Dunnett
Drought-tolerant planting

This type of planting is about making the right choice of plants as well as creating the appropriate growing conditions for them. Growing plants 'hard' – in free-draining soils that have had very little organic matter incorporated, and at closer spacings than might normally be considered – will make them tough, stress tolerant and naturally better able to withstand harsh conditions. Good, reliable, drought-tolerant plants that all work well in a naturalistic mix together include *Dianthus carthusianorum, Stachys byzantina, Erodium manescavii, Oenothera macrocarpa, Sedum telephium* 'Purple Emperor', *Limonium platyphyllum, Gaura lindheimeri, Phlomis russeliana, Stipa tenuissima* and *Verbascum phoeniceum.*

[left] The bold leaves of succulent (and therefore drought-tolerant) *Agave americana* give a strong focal point to this planting.

[below left] Bright pink flowers of *Erodium manescavii* bring a vivid and warm feeling to the front of the border.

[below] This silver-leaved *Stachys*, which survives substantial drought and heat, is neatly contained by this attractive edging. Its sprawling habit would otherwise eventually envelop the path.

A nod to a natural style

The naturalistic planting style has been gaining pace over the last 15 years or so. In its loosest form, it involves designing with plants that mimic associations and styles found in nature – but by using ornamental cultivated plants rather than only natives. Thus, many schemes will include swathes of plants growing together, seeming to entwine as they might in nature. This style is relatively easy to recreate – if you have the space – but beware that even though it may look impromptu it does take substantial foresight and skill to achieve. One of the primary concerns is that of how the plants will grow together over time; the gardener needs to monitor and intervene (if necessary) to ensure a balance is maintained. Chelsea gardens provide great ideas for naturalistic planting, but if recreating them in your garden be sure to know what plants you are selecting and how they will develop.

ALL IN THE MIX

A range of flowering and foliage plants can combine to produce a naturalistic feel in a planting scheme.

1 In this large naturalistic design the plants have been allowed to grow closely together while retaining individual form and colour. The long thin leaves of purple *Phormium*, the nodding heads of the grass *Stipa gigantea* and the soft yellow-cream flowers of *Achillea* mix to good effect.

2 A mass of white *Geranium phaeum* **'Album'**, flanked on the right by spires of white *Digitalis*, lead the garden visitor's eye through the space, to the silver birch tree trunks beyond.

3 Yellow-and-white wetland *Iris* exude light and colour in this planting area, which borders and provides definition to the paving to the left. The different flower and leaf shapes make an overall impression similar to combinations found in nature.

4 Rivers of colour and texture abound in this show garden, but a large space would be needed in a home garden to achieve such a result. Its blend of silver-leaved *Stachys byzantina*, the purple rounded heads of *Allium*, the purple spires of *Salvia* and the creamy yellow *Achillea* beyond conjure an almost prairie feel. The bold dash of red in the centre brings a natural disharmony to the scene.

Containers for all gardens

As garden design has developed over the years, so too have the products and artefacts to support it. Containers and planters are no exception to this evolution. By using improved manufacturing techniques and new materials, a wealth of ideas has been developed for containers. In addition to this, increasing plant availability and choice have meant a wider range of species can be grown in planters. Containers, however, are man-made environments, so you must consider your plant choice carefully as well as each plant's ability to grow in a restricted space and whether you can maintain the effect you desire. There are practical considerations, too, when planting in containers. Good-quality potting compost must be used; feeding, especially during periods of strong growth, must be done; water-retaining gel can be used; and watering, even in times of rain, should be monitored and checked.

EYE-CATCHING STATEMENTS

Dramatic planters can be used as really strong design statements in a garden, but ensure plants can live happily with their bedfellows.

1 This unusual scheme by a Japanese designer used a series of large 'containers' at different levels to accentuate the form and texture of each plant. The same plants have been grouped in each planter, helping reinforce a bold but restrained vision of a contained garden.

2 Variegated *Euonymus*, yellow-leaved *Heuchera* and mixed pansies create a co-ordinated display in these containers, perched on poles standing more than 2m (6½ft) tall.

3 The bright summer colour of *Calendula* lifts this corner of the garden, while the massive container underneath acts in a supporting but defining role.

NO NEED FOR PLANTS

Not all planters or containers have to be filled with plants. Sometimes their beauty can be appreciated better when they are left empty.

1 A glazed urn has been placed on its side to reduce its overall impact, while the flowering *Rhododendron* around it helps to give context – and a focal point – to the scene.

2 In this classic take on garden design, a row of pots, atop sturdy and almost over-sized plinths, stand proud and consistent. The beauty of their shape defies the convention for planting up a container.

EXPERT TIP
Tom Stuart-Smith
Cloud pruning

❛ 'Cloud pruning' is a brilliantly expressive term as it describes the process exactly, that is, pruning any plant to resemble a cumulus in its full buxom splendour. This technique is normally done on box and yew. The idea of cloud pruning a tree is based on the Japanese tradition of Niwaki, in which the tree is pruned to reveal and accentuate its essential form and branch structure. When used *en masse*, cloud pruning can give a slightly surreal and dreamy impression. ❜

When trimming plants, swivel-blade hand shears are useful for giving a precise finish – in this case, to a box (*Buxus*) ball.

Cloud pruning is not an easy task, and takes years of dedicated pruning and foresight to achieve such an end result. Mature examples such as this, however, can be found for sale in garden centres.

SUCCESS IN SIMPLICITY

Often just one or two types of plants can be used to great effect in some schemes; thus, less can be better than more in a container.

1 Basket-weave terracotta pots have been planted with pink-purple *Osteospermum* (on the left) and silver-leaved *Convolvulus cneorum* (on the right). When viewed in combination with the planting surrounding them, they make a great overall garden scene.

2 Bay is a popular choice for many gardeners, as its evergreen leaves provide year-round foliage, plus it can also be easily shaped or trained. Here the trunks have been twisted slightly for a spiral effect.

3 This old washing tub makes a good base for an alpine-type display, filled with *Sempervivum* and stones. These succulents are great for containers as they need little additional watering.

4 Clean and stark planters, filled with a white mulch, are welcome homes to *Libertia grandiflora*, the tall white flower spires of which give an elegance and stature to the display.

5 In this great fun and sustainable way to recycle an old item, succulents (*Sempervivum* and *Echeveria* selections) almost take over the old tool box. The pretty flowering stems of the *Echeveria* seem to dance in the air.

5

THE DAILY TELEGRAPH GARDEN

Often at Chelsea the outside gardens tackle the topic of planting head-on. In this instance, Belgian-born Isabelle Van Groeningen and her partner German-born Gabriella Pape explored planting combinations and ecological understanding. They focused on the renowned plant breeder Karl Foerster, who died in his native Germany in 1970. He was a master in plant breeding, whether summer-flowering delphiniums, salvias or cottage-garden campanulas; during his lifetime he bred and selected in excess of 600 new plants. This design, however, is based on a strong, formal structure and shows just what can be achieved when considered, sublime planting is set into a simple overall shape.

Foerster's lifelong passion for perennials reflected a man who wrote, encouraged others and undertook endless refinement of his chosen subjects. In this garden, the designers have done much the same: plant combinations are inspired by Foerster's sunken garden at Potsdam-Bornim. They also, like so many other Chelsea gardeners, show how different horticultural thinking can be applied at home. Take, for example, the way the plants have been placed, by dividing the planting into three styles. The first is traditional border plantings, with low plants at the front and taller ones at the rear; the second is drift planting (behind the pond), where shapes and colours grow together; and the third style is 'mingled' or 'tapestry' planting, where colours and textures are interwoven.

THEIR DESIGN ALSO BENEFITS FROM MANY OTHER CLEVER IDEAS:

- by creating a sunken space, the garden feels much bigger than it actually is – this is an easy technique to employ at home if you manage to find room to use the soil you have dug out;
- the overall design is simple and strong – rectangular and linear. It doesn't try to do too much, but lets the planting be the centre of attention;
- even in smaller gardens, different areas can be created – take, for example, the seating area on the left of the garden or the pergola running along the back;
- dark green hedges (both yew and box) are used to help contain the exuberant planting and to give the visitor's eye something restful to settle on; it also provides winter structure when much of this planting would be under ground;
- colour theming – whether it be flowers or hard materials – is important, and care has been given to make sure colours either sit well together or contrast strongly.

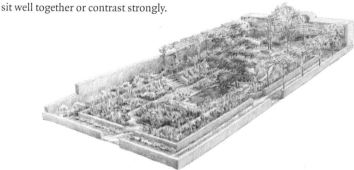

1 A hedge is crucial for providing a backdrop to much floral delight in a fairly small area. The clean lines of the yew (*Taxus baccata*) and its deep shade of green are in contrast to the rest of the planting.

2 The white bench plays a vital role: its colour ties in with the climbing rose as well as the foxgloves and other white flowers. It also allows the visitor to view, from a vantage point, the planting below, and it helps break up the length of the left side of the garden.

DESIGNER Isabelle Van Groeningen and Gabriella Pape

CONTRACTOR Crocus.co.uk

AWARD Silver-Gilt Flora

CATEGORY Show Garden, 2007

SPONSOR Telegraph Media Group

KEY WORDS plants; German; continental influence; abundant colours; sunken

IN A SENTENCE... A densely planted garden that shows beautiful plant combinations held together in a simple but strong ground plan.

3 The addition of a pergola in any garden is often a great choice – it brings height to a space, creates light and shade and allows a different range of plants to be grown. Here, the designers have successfully mixed white *Rosa* 'Bobbie James' with purple *Wisteria sinensis*.

4 This is a really planterly garden, with stunning combinations giving a feeling of warmth and early summer. In the 'tapestry'-type area, the orange-reds of geums mix with purple-flowered *Salvia* x *sylvestris* 'Mainacht', *S. nemorosa* 'Caradonna', *S. n.* 'Ostfriesland' and creamy yellow *Aquilegia chrysantha* 'Yellow Queen'. The result is full-on colour.

5 A contemporary feel has been included by this brushed steel sculpture homage to Karl Foerster by Simon Packard. It was inspired by grasses, and helps the visitor's eye focus on an end point in the garden. Imagine if it wasn't there – there would be so much 'flower power' your eye wouldn't know where to look; with this sculpture a sense of visual direction is achieved.

THE LAURENT-PERRIER GARDEN

There is often a temptation to include too many colours or 'elements' in a garden, in a vain attempt to make it look more exciting. This one is a successful essay in how to do the complete opposite. Simple textures, a range of form and plant shape, and a repetitious use of the colour green, are bisected by rectangular paving setts and raised zinc tanks of water. The design balances masses (planting, water troughs) and voids (spaces between trees, paths), and allows the entity to work as one while still giving discrete areas for walking or sitting. The result is a cool, subtle and pared-down statement of what a garden can be.

Tom Stuart-Smith is a well-known Chelsea designer who always manages to succeed in creating awe-inspiring show gardens, as he also does for his many private clients. He described this grove as 'a contemplative space with a dreamy, slightly surreal character'... and with good reason.

CONSIDER THE QUALITY OF THIS SPACE:

- the cool and constant 'base notes' of the groundcovering greens, in leaf shape and flower form;
- the sporadic punctuation of white flowers;
- trimmed, 30-year-old, 'cloud-pruned' hornbeams that give height, maturity and structure;
- a seemingly random planting pattern held within organic border shapes;
- water features, an end wall and paving that bring man-made materials to an otherwise planterly space.

At home, such refined choices might be difficult to make – you need a focused planting palette and a high level of maintenance to keep the consistency that is shown in these photographs. Also, much of this planting would die down during winter months. Remember this garden was on display for only six days, not six months or even six years! However, it shows how less can often mean more: with some choice (and often expensive) focal points (here, hornbeam trees and water features), and with a matrix of planting underneath softening the effect, a garden of calm and the designer's slight 'surrealism' can be achieved.

Seemingly random planting in this cool and contemplative garden gives a lush informal feel (left). It is protectively watched over by cloud-pruned hornbeams – dominating but also framing the space. The zinc troughs of water – from a distance looking black and bottomless – bring an extra dimension.

1 These zinc tanks are a perfect example of high-quality detailing adding to the overall effect of a garden. A small gap between the surface level of the water and the edge of the tanks allows water to spill over and recirculate. The gap is consistent; the water is level (and black lined which helps give a feeling of 'the unknown'); and the combination of colours (black and silver) is contemporary and complementary. Such sublime detailing helps any garden exude a feeling of quality and longevity.

DESIGNER Tom Stuart-Smith

CONTRACTOR Crocus.co.uk

AWARD Gold; Best in Show

CATEGORY Show Garden, 2008

SPONSOR Laurent-Perrier

KEY WORDS green; texture; cloud-pruned hornbeams; refined; calming; grove

IN A SENTENCE... Sublime place-making using a simple palette of materials and colours.

2 Looking along the linear Flemish paving setts of the path you can see how the proportion of the planting either side neither dominates nor underwhelms – the balance is spot on. This garden is a lesson in what should go into, and stay out of, a designed space.

3 Trees cloud-pruned within a centimetre of their lives give a rounded and structural feel to the garden. This sculptural, large-scale bonsai treatment adds to the densely planted, green grove. If you were to try this at home, it would take you decades to achieve; if you want the look, it may be best to blow the budget and buy mature examples like these, but they aren't your normal garden-centre finds.

4 Three oversized domes of box (*Buxus*) in containers give a regimented but defined feel to the back wall – and a sense of form and structure for the visitor to look towards – among all the greenery and seamless planting in this garden.

5 The combination of small rounded leaves of *Asarum europaeum* near to wide-leaved, toothed rodgersias, white-flowering astrantias, small-leaved hostas and other groundcovering plants creates a mainly green, textural and dense vegetative design.

OUTDOOR LIVING

The possibilities for living how you want, in your garden, are truly endless.

Most people who are interested in gardening, in whatever form, enjoy being outdoors whether it is for nurturing unusual types of plants or sharing a glass of wine with friends, for giving children the opportunity to run amok or for walking around an arboretum full of enormous trees. It is unsurprising therefore that the concept of 'outdoor living' is so firmly rooted in people's minds.

In the garden design world, the term 'outdoor living' loosely covers dining areas, patios, decks, outdoor kitchens, spaces for the kids to play and so on. However, if Chelsea and the other gardening shows across the world teach us one thing, it is that gardening is one of the most diverse pastimes you can find. Just as everyone is different, so too are their gardens – and their 'outdoor living' space.

But what Chelsea does better than most shows, perhaps, is demonstrate just what you may want from your space. In essence, it concerns anything that you might see built or sitting in your garden – from outdoor kitchens to concealed lighting, from exterior paint to shade structures. This chapter specifically focuses on elements such as buildings, unusual features, seating and changing uses of your garden. (In reality, of course, elements such as paving, entrances, paths and walls would also be included, but these are dealt with in chapter 4.)

At its largest, outdoor living considers the role of garden buildings, as well as more subtle garden structures. Garden rooms, whether wooden summerhouses or brick-built architectural statements, have always been part of a garden's recipe, but only in the past 20 or 30 years has there been an explosion of design style and material choice. Designers now create their own garden room or structure to sit in harmony with the overall design. For gardeners, many similar buildings are available to purchase from specialist firms. Equally, if your taste and budget are less flamboyant, then sheds, summerhouses, greenhouses and other garden rooms can be made by a competent builder, or put together by a DIY enthusiast.

Garden features, on the other hand, seem to be a whole new design development. They work in so many ways that not even designers can really define them, but their benefit is often undoubted. Some may be small pods for sitting or resting in; others may provide a subtle amount of shading; a few may be physical entities that help frame a view or the overall design. More often than not such features are used in a contemporary, modern, quite pared-down way, but that should not restrict your imagination. In a domestic setting, for example, you may think that an awning hanging above your patio doors is a little dated, and that a large patio umbrella is not big enough. The garden structure you may end up with could be a hybrid between a pergola joined to a horizontal trellis but made out of painted metal. It is features such as these

2

1 The shape of the cubed seats relates well to the box hedging surrounding them. Such a relationship between plants and built structures is vital.

2 For many people, gardens are for relaxing in. Seating therefore is essential and must not only be comfortable but also visually link in with the overall design.

3 If a particular style or culture inspires you, then consider all elements from planting to seating, containers to wall colour. The more authentic these elements are, the more convincing the end result.

4 'Outdoor rooms' are increasingly being created by designers, either as guest rooms, work spaces or play areas for children. Their architecture, as is so well achieved here, must be thought through carefully.

1

3

4

that are really exciting – you can't always put your finger on what they are or exactly what they do, but you know that the design would be a lot weaker without them.

From individual chairs that blend into the background through to bold and dramatic 'design statements', where and how you sit is an essential part of anyone's use of their outside space. Something that has really developed in recent years, however, has been the outdoor sofa (see p90) – or even 'sun bed'.

Increasingly, gardeners are considering climate change. Nowhere is this more true than in the creations from Fleming's Nurseries of Australia, whose outdoor kitchens (with integral barbecue and cooker; see case study, p100) give a taster as to what would be possible if climate change became particularly advanced for cool-temperate gardeners.

So what does this range of outdoor living examples provide? It demonstrates inspiration and ideas. It shows that if you need a building in your back yard, why not do something different. It shows that if you want new materials, then get thinking. But above all it

gives people confidence to try techniques, combinations and styles that they may not be aware of. Much of this wouldn't have been possible without Chelsea leading the way, showing what can be done in the garden. The possibilities for living how you want, in your garden, are truly endless.

Sitting pretty, sitting well

Out of all the hard landscaping elements considered for a garden, seating is perhaps of most significant value. A comfortable seat, whether for an individual or for many, can help a garden visitor truly relax in an outside space, reinforcing the relationship between gardener and garden. The location, style, material and size of the seats must be appropriate to the garden in general, and can be temporary or long-term, home-made or shop-bought. Bear in mind also the demands of seat maintenance and upkeep, and practical issues of mowing regimes or surrounding planting. Seating comes in all shapes and sizes, so there should always be something for every garden. In addition to more conventional seating, bespoke and off-the-shelf benches are possible, especially for the more social gardeners, allowing more people to enjoy the garden space.

BLENDING INTO THE BACKGROUND

Not all seats need be bold or obvious; sometimes the really successful ones have a supporting role.

1 A simple wooden bench sits quietly in some dense planting, and offers an area of respite for the garden visitor from which to contemplate the plants and water feature beyond.

2 These chairs complement the overall design of the garden, blending pretty planting with rustic hard landscaping materials, as well as giving the impression of a romantic, cottage-garden outside space.

STATEMENT CHAIRS

Whether introduced singly or in pairs, chairs are a crucial element in the outside space.

1 These contemporary moulded chairs give a luxurious feel to this 'room', by matching not only the colours of the paving and the white of the flowers, but also by having purple cushions, which tie in with the table and wall colour.

2 White mesh 'daisy'-like seats bring some humour and visual interest to this garden. Their transparent nature makes the space feel bigger.

3 This large stone plinth, cut smooth on the top and left textured on its side, acts both as a seat and as a physical mass between planting.

4 Complementing the Chinese style of this show garden, the designer has allocated this quiet corner for resting and drinking tea.

This garden combines a feeling of spaciousness with modernity, by its use of a reinforced glass flooring overlaid on water that runs down the curved wall towards the seating area. Using your outside space in such a way is becoming increasingly popular where open space is limited.
The Witan Wisdom Garden, Nicholas Dexter, 2009

Benches for different uses

The facility for more than one person to sit down and enjoy a garden is increasingly being explored (see also p90). For this, benches are becoming important and now comprise a significant proportion of garden furniture, welcoming as they are for conversation, lying on or making a design statement. However, as can be seen in the examples illustrated here, benches are also becoming integral to the built form of the garden, whether as visual 'relief' to planting, part retaining wall or as artworks in their own right. The upshot is that the bench so often associated with public parks or bus shelters is long gone – now is the age of new ideas, whatever your requirements.

SHARP AND STRAIGHT

Linear benches add more than just a place to sit in a garden; they provide a strong design statement, too.

1 These black timber benches not only create a physical barrier between path and planting, but also add texture and colour to this attractive scene.

2 A solid limestone, L-shaped bench defines the corner of this urban garden while providing a well-sized seating facility.

3 This timber cantilevered bench is a great idea for a small garden: it is comfortable and attractive, and the space underneath allows for shade-loving plants to establish.

PART OF THE PLAN

For a scheme's ultimate success it is often important to consider how and where your bench will reside in a garden.

1 Enticing people to stop en route along the path is this glass, steel and timber sculptural seat, which also acts as a strong focal point.

2 Benches can be pieces of art in their own right. Here, the designer has blended the practical requirement of somewhere to sit with the artistic desire to link the bench visually into the overall design idea.

3 A long, curved concrete bench forms part of the retaining wall for the planting behind (see also p48). It looks great whether or not it is being used by people as a place to sit and have refreshments.

Taking your sofa outside

As Chelsea designers have looked further afield for inspiration, so too have they developed new ideas. One such is the advent of the garden 'sofa' – not always technically a sofa, but certainly a seating device that has the traits of settee, day bed or lounging area. The sofa concept is to encourage gardeners to relax, use and surround themselves with their plants or a view; the upshot, however, is a great conduit for conversation and entertainment. The reality for many gardeners is that they may not have enough space to incorporate such a feature, plus there is the realistic practicality of taking the cushions in and out when dodging poor weather. Yet, when executed well and established in the appropriate place, sofas can make a really unusual and welcome addition to outdoor living.

EXPERT TIP
Bunny Guinness
Creating a conversation pit

‘When seated comfortably in a sunken and contained sitting area, somehow the setting is always more conducive to great conversations. Lowering the space increases the sense of intimacy, and on the practical side makes it more sheltered and cosy. If you add a central firepit for warmth, you may well be deep in conversation long into the night. In such a sunken area, you can design or build your own furniture more simply and still make it look über-chic. I love really wide seats – ones that you can sit on with your legs and feet tucked under you. By using large cushions you can add dramatic swatches of colour to the scene. Slot in an outdoor projector and you can even watch films outside. If there is no convenient wall, just hang up a temporary white sheet. ’

Steps lead down to a sunken seating area, with illuminated water feature, offering a place for informal relaxation and conversation.

THE FURNISHING TOUCH

Outdoor sofas must suit your overall garden design and are available in all shapes and sizes.

1 Taking its inspiration directly from interior furniture designers, this scheme mimics the common domestic arrangement in a sitting room – of a sofa being placed against a wall, in front of a fire, and augmented with scatter cushions.

2 This relaxing area, surrounded by soft pink busy Lizzie bedding plants, is more of a chill-out, cushioned hollow than a sofa.

3 A suspended, almost futuristic relaxing 'pod' has been softened by white cushions; the fact that it has sides and a roof also helps to give garden visitors a sense of privacy and enclosure.

4 This clever design uses a sweeping timber screen wall to house a day bed that could be pulled out or pushed in as the users desire.

This outside living space has myriad ideas: from the long sofa seat backed by the striated stone retaining walls, to the 'plug hole' water feature and the smooth interplay between water level and decking. The end result is a truly relaxing place.

Fleming's and Trailfinders Australian Garden, presented by Melbourne, Victoria, Jamie Durie, 2008

Shade and structure

Introducing a structural element to a design is common for many Chelsea designers – the built form adding an air of permanence and solidity. In a domestic garden, the addition of some type of shade or physical structure has an equally important benefit, as well as meeting that deep-seated human desire to be protected and shielded. The design of such structures can take cues from modernist buildings or Chinese tea houses, rustic ironworks or glass rooms. Sometimes the role can be practical protection; at other times it can allude to a physical presence but is in fact more about style and stage-set. The use of garden structures can be permanent or seasonal, fully functional or light hearted. Whatever end result is chosen doesn't really matter, although as a garden owner you must consider what you need this building to achieve and how its inclusion can be adapted to your site.

INTEGRITY IN STRUCTURE

Physical forms are often important parts of Chelsea gardens and, if budget and space allow, could also be in home gardens.

1 This modern design was inspired by Japanese architecture, and it features an acrylic roof and end wall that houses ceramic sculptures by Japanese artist Mari-Ruth Oda.

2 Simple white screens, used both vertically and horizontally, help to create a series of defined spaces within this garden.

3 A substantial structure, such as this, is a bold statement for any designer, but when used with conviction could be introduced into a home garden.

1

2

3

4

PERSONAL SPACE

Including areas in a garden that feel personal and 'human scale' is important for people's enjoyment.

1 A quiet corner has been established here, and the deck is large enough for a small table and chairs; note the angled water features fronting the timber side walls, which add a nice touch.

2 With its hints of Oriental gardens mixed with savannah grassland, this deck (with roof) makes for an easily replicable garden element.

3 These sunken white pods work in harmony with the mounds of planting while giving garden visitors somewhere to relax.

4 For many, an outdoor structure under which they can eat and entertain friends is a crucial requirement for their garden, and such structures can be beautiful additions.

5 A 'rib-cage' timber hut has been cleverly used to enliven an otherwise dull corner of a garden.

5

Garden buildings for all styles

Installing or commissioning a garden building can be a costly exercise for a gardener, and may well include requiring planning permission and substantial earthworks. However such constraints should not undermine in any way the enormous beauty and long-term benefit a building can bring. In essence, it symbolises that the garden owner is in control of the space, that he or she means to stay there for some time. This act of permanence is a reminder of someone's love for their outside space; it is a visable commitment to their land. There are many different types of structures available, some shop-bought while others require architectural endeavour. Consider how often the structure is to be used; what it needs to deliver; and ongoing maintenance costs. Whatever your choice, its inclusion can bring a whole new energy and visual enjoyment to your outside garden.

TRADITIONAL TAKE

A range of styles and designs can link a property with its surrounding architecture or with a considered reference to days gone by.

1 Buildings such as this one form the backdrop to many a famous historical garden, and bring elegance and architectural interest that complements the surrounding planting.

2 A simple summerhouse, well painted and gentrified inside, is a realistic addition to a Chelsea garden that many gardeners would aspire to having; note the wisteria climbing up one side.

3 Although stylised and even quite kitsch, this evocation of a beach hut is well executed and could easily be accommodated in the right garden.

THE ROOM OUTSIDE

Actual buildings in which to house offices or guest suites are increasingly being constructed in the garden by people who want more living space.

1 Garden rooms should be practical, useful and beautiful. This contemporary summerhouse provides a great enclosed room, and has a washing line that can be folded away and hidden behind out of sight.

2 The low-slung shape and soft-toned materials used in this building allow it to bed in well with the planting in the garden – light shines into it from the glass windows, connecting inside to outside.

3 Green roofs – designed and constructed to support living plants – are increasingly being used in private and public schemes, and they help give visual garden interest as well as biodiversity a boost.

Outside space with something different

So much of gardening relates to how the individual personalises his or her outdoor space. Whether it is a certain combination of plants that reflect personal preference, or an array of materials that indicate different travels, a garden can be developed to make specific or oblique reference to the creator's desire. With this in mind, how a gardener 'decorates' the space should be considered in conjunction with any hard or soft landscaping that is needed to ensure

the desired look will still be created as the scheme nears completion. For Chelsea designers, such examples of decorative touches include bespoke sculpture, ingenious practical ideas and whimsical suggestions, and these can inspire gardeners into thinking harder about what could go into their garden. With a dash of creativity and confidence, supported by practical skills, a range of different ideas can be achieved.

5

EXPERT TIP
Bunny Guinness
Dressing the garden for a party

' One of the most satisfactory ways of creating a celebratory feeling is to introduce large terracotta (or other) pots with water buckets hidden inside filled with massive bouquets of flowers or with generous sprigs of greenery spiced up with any readily available flowers. Position these in prominent places to frame the front gate or door, or raise them up either side of a flight of steps for big impact. For a makeshift awning, create a loosely woven rectangle of coloured-ribbon hessian or similar and hang it between four convenient trees or partially hook it to a wall or fence; you could even rig it up on poles. This simple adornment will make any outside eating area special, however large or small. Fairy lights, cushions and candles are essential, while table runners add colour. You could also dot sprigs of cut lavender on the table. '

PERSONAL PREFERENCE

A range of elements can be included in a garden to respond to a gardener's aesthetic or practical needs.

1 A clever outdoor cupboard gives space for composting and recycling, and has a herb trough planted on top of it.

2 Taking the concept of the edible garden to the extreme, the designers here used every available space for growing fruit or vegetables.

3 This garden, designed for a biker, was envisaged to be situated at the back of a garage, offering a place for escape. Bike parts, oil drums and old tyres are all included in the scene.

4 Two bikes outside the front door of a house use the space efficiently and are readily accessible.

5 Even though not every garden has space for such a building, this beautiful dovecote acts as a strong focal point to the back of this space. Its colour provides relief to the shadow of the trees.

[above] Simple small details, such as this candle hanging in a jar decorated with a checked ribbon, can really help personalise a plot.

[left] Fairy lights can extend a garden's use into night-time, while adding a fun party atmosphere.

FLEMING'S NURSERIES AUSTRALIAN GARDEN PRESENTED BY TRAILFINDERS

Because Australia's climate is so very different from that of the UK's it is difficult to see what commonalities gardens from the two countries may have. Of course, planting, hard landscaping, spatial division, water features and attention to detail are human requirements that transcend the globe, not climates, but it is perhaps their use of space that is fundamentally different. Australians are renowned for their love of the outdoors, cooking outside and using plants and structures to provide shade, and this has inspired Chelsea visitors (and designers) to re-evaluate their own outside space and what they want to do in it.

The concept of outdoor living was not new – indeed John Brookes, the leading gardening light from the 1960s, coined the phrase the 'outdoor room'. But this garden, by Dean Herald, opened our eyes still further by incorporating a cooking environment surrounded by stunning planting, a fascinating water feature and bold architectural statements. In his brief the designer explained that the garden 'provides a complete, tailored Australian outdoor lifestyle experience... [which] is both practical and ornamental, catering for the whole family'.

ELEMENTS THAT ARE EASY TO TAKE INTO YOUR GARDEN:

- the concept of including a kitchen area which allows for the garden to become a complete entertaining space;
- stonework is often an expensive and labour-intensive addition to any garden, but, as here, it provides a dramatic focal point for visitors to the space;
- bold, architectural planting, along with a muted palette of whites and greens, gives a cool and calming feel; it also allows for the hard landscaping materials to be more varied in colour and texture;
- water flowing through the glass-top table (suspended from a stone wall) and landing into a pool creates a stunning effect;
- by using various levels and different angles to great effect, the space seems much bigger and more interesting than its actual dimensions would suggest;
- the concept of outdoor living can really be pushed to the limit: not many designers would include a sofa (along with cushions) and outdoor fireplace, but this space demonstrates just what can be considered.

1 A dedicated dining table has been included to help get maximum value out of this space. The seating for six surrounds a bespoke glass-topped, water feature table (see inset). Trees behind provide screening and shading.

2 A low, long, box hedge divides the path from the sunken seating area and adds a dash of bright green. Such a traditional design element can work well in a contemporary garden, but beware of mixing too many styles.

Designer Dean Herald

Contractor Rolling Stone Landscapes

Award Gold

Category Show Garden, 2006

Sponsor Fleming's Nurseries, Trailfinders

Key words contemporary; outdoor living; stonework; seating; linear; kitchen

In a sentence... A cool and well-composed design for a garden that has entertaining and family fun at its heart.

3 Outdoor sofas invite the visitor to sit back and relax. Cushions soften the effect and reinforce the 'outdoor living' theme; note also the 'coffee table' with associated ornaments. Just as when you are decorating the rooms inside your house, such styling and decoration should be considered for convincing outside living.

4 Paving is treated simply in this garden, with regular stone, grey square slabs running the main width of the garden, but here it is interrupted by reinforced glass. The effect not only visually breaks up the long path, but also links the glass with the same colour used on the outdoor dining table at the end of the garden.

5 Wooden logs have been given their own space in this wall, adding to the dramatic shape, texture and colour of the contrasting stonework. They also have a practical use here, as they are near to the outdoor fireplace.

6 The stone wall gives a dramatic backdrop to the seating area and hides the kitchen and cooking space beyond. The colour variation in the stone is a neat use of a natural material, making the space feel lighter and texturally more interesting. When designing your garden, you should consider how materials look individually and *en masse*.

ECO CHIC

Look around any city or town and you will often see little 'pockets' of spaces – land that developers forgot, that has slipped by without anyone really noticing. Such a premise has inspired many a designer, and often with fantastic results. In urban spaces, every centimetre counts. Just such a space featured in the 2009 RHS Chelsea Flower Show: Kate Gould's 'Eco Chic' was a subtle blend of environmental awareness with stylish design. Gardeners are increasingly wanting their space (whether rural or urban) to be stylish yet functional, contemporary yet environmentally considerate, useful yet attractive, and such design ideas found in this small area can help you realise your dreams in your own garden.

Balancing chic, contemporary design with recycled or reclaimed materials can often be a challenge – by their very nature they are not usual bedfellows. But in this garden, the designer managed to achieve a great harmony. The premise of the design had 'a pronounced eco edge' to it, by using discarded elements often left behind by builders and contractors. It was assumed that this garden was overlooked by surrounding buildings (often a reality in an urban environment) so planting was shade tolerant and continued up the wall to help reduce the visual impact of man-made materials. There really was a plethora of ideas in this space that can be taken to any garden, in any location – the fact that it was so convincing as a small, urban garden added to its appeal.

OTHER CONSIDERATIONS TO NOTE:

- the hard landscaping is permeable, so as to make use of every available drop of rain that might enter the space, as well as capturing and reusing 'grey water' from the adjacent buildings;
- the balance of materials is significant: the designer reused scaffold poles and boards, as well as introduced industrial materials such as expanded mesh walkways and glass panel screens;
- a water feature runs partially down the back wall, giving visual interest and movement, as well as helping block out surrounding noise;
- the visitor has a defined access point into the space (following a predetermined route often allows the designer to maximise all available space) and, in addition, level changes make the space feel much bigger;
- a 'living' wall softens the whole back wall and gives visual interest throughout the year; walls like these are becoming increasingly popular in show gardens and will soon become more so in domestic schemes.

1 Recessed, mirror-polished, stainless steel panels reflect available light and give a sense of depth to the space – just what you want in a tiny urban garden. This is typical of the ingenious little tricks that have been used so cleverly in this space.

2 Scaffold boards and poles have been thoroughly cleaned to emphasise the 'chic' look and make the best use of available materials. As a sensible precaution, a hardwood top board protects the softwood below.

DESIGNER Kate Gould

CONTRACTOR The Garden Builders

AWARD Gold; Best Urban Garden

CATEGORY Urban Garden, 2009

SPONSOR Helios

KEY WORDS stylish; urban space; angular; mixture of textures; 'living' wall; recycled materials

IN A SENTENCE... A great example of what you can achieve in any space by considering material selection, changing levels and planting combinations.

3 A beautifully shaped *Acer palmatum* brings colour and a soft texture to this 'hard' space and makes a central focal point. Planting has been considered carefully here. On the assumption that there are buildings on all sides, the chosen plants are shade tolerant, don't mind some sporadic damp or drought conditions and are generally considered pretty tough.

4 Permeable paving has been used to allow water to pass through and so make best use of all available water; any excess is captured and reused. Note also the physical fact that the visitor has to step down onto the paving, thereby giving the illusion of extra space.

5 'Living' walls are becoming increasingly popular in show gardens. There is still some work to be done by the industry to see how long such plantings can survive, and how much irrigation/maintenance they need, but their concept is to be welcomed. The main advantage of living walls is that they provide plenty of softness without taking up precious floor space. With the correct plant selection and establishment, their role should become increasingly significant in bringing greenery to cities everywhere.

6 A bench has been cantilevered to maintain an air gap beneath. Such seating is paramount to getting the most out of any outdoor space.

WATER

By working with many of the world's most ingenious water specialists, Chelsea designers have produced some truly memorable creations.

Of all elements that can be incorporated into a garden design, it is perhaps water that tests most gardeners. No such worries concern the designers at Chelsea, however, where the role and application of water has come on in leaps and bounds. The range of water effects will open your eyes to just what is possible, but the challenge can be to choose the most appropriate for your garden.

Over the years, all manner of water features have been on display at Chelsea – from natural-looking ponds, through long formal rills, to water apparently running uphill. Some creations are true 'statement' pieces, where shock and awe are the intention; others add a softer tone. Shapes and sizes abound, with raised troughs looking as good as stepped ponds; natural cascades comparing favourably with fountains and jets; simple urns with a trickle of water adding as much to a scheme as an infinity-edge swimming pool.

For many garden schemes the inclusion of a water feature is an integral part of the design: whether on the ground plan or vertical, without water the space would fail to work. It is perhaps in these schemes, where water plays as crucial a role as a tree or patio, that you can start to consider why water gardening in your private garden needs care and attention. Considering many different issues will help you focus your requirements.

Not only do the Chelsea gardens show you big or small, modern or traditional, simple or complicated water gardening, but they also provide you with tricks of the trade. Take the colour black, for example. Not a natural water colour, yet 'black' ponds nearly always feature. There are two main ways of creating the effect: by lining the pond structure with a taut black plastic, or by painting the sides and bottom black; or, for a short-term effect, dye is added to the water to make it black. Whichever way is chosen, an illusion of depth is created. Many of the water features may be just 30cm (12in) deep,

but by making them black the viewer is tricked into thinking they are something bigger.

Reflection is also a key factor for many designers: flat calm water often creates a different atmosphere in the space, reflecting light, clouds, sun, trees and so on. Other conceits employed, which can be easily mirrored in a domestic setting, include: tying in (or contrasting) the colour of the pool or pond with paving, fencing or planting; lighting certain parts of the water body (such as a fountain or rill) to extend its visual appeal into the evening; and adding misting machines that can lend an air of mystery and the fantastical to a creation.

MAKING WATER WORK

Ponds and water features range from rain-fed seasonal ponds, through off-the-shelf water features to large-scale pools or ponds or formal water channels such as rills. Whatever you desire, make sure you know how the effect will work in your garden, and research water gardening in detail. Look at magazines, books or open gardens for inspiration. If in any doubt, you can consult your local pond or water specialist. Consider also the need for any pumping or electricity: remember that only qualified electricians can bring an electricity supply into your garden.

FIRST STEPS TO WATER GARDENING

Including water in your home garden can be a big decision, so consider your responses to some of these necessary questions:

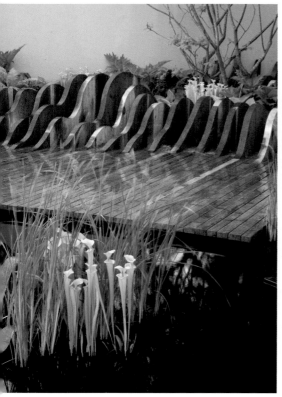

3

- Why do you want water?
- What role is it playing and what is it adding to your space?
- Do you want something that will block out noise, or is it more a visual requirement, such as adding movement?
- Should the water be flat or uneven?
- Is the water for interacting with (getting into it and getting wet) or is it something that you would prefer to view from a certain distance?
- Is safety an issue (especially with younger children or pets)?
- How will wildlife benefit from including a water garden in your scheme?
- Does the feature need electricity to make it work (pump and lighting, for example)?
- How much maintenance will it require each year to make it look as good as intended?
- Are you wanting a small, floor-mounted water feature bought from a local shop or does your idea require building works or planning regulations?

- Do you need a deep structure, or can you get away with a much more shallow effect?
- Will you need specialist advice to make your desire become a reality?

Clearly, the answers to these questions aren't always going to be straightforward, but if you can't answer them yet you may need more consideration time. The larger the water feature, the less forgiving the end result will be if you have not thought the plan through.

Water really can bring a new dimension to any garden, be it large or small, rural or urban. But careful siting, consideration of how the effect will be created and the need for ongoing maintenance, make water features less of an impulse buy than some might consider. There is a style of water gardening to suit all tastes and a wide range of budgets, so do not hurry your decision. However, after exploring the range of designs over the next few pages, your imagination is the one thing the water feature in your garden never need lack.

1 Dark water in close proximity to a timber deck and wooden 'waves' is a reference to the fragile nature of the world's bogs. Although the water is still, the sculptures provides movement.

2 Most designers like to include water in their gardens because of the variety of benefits it can bring – colour, sound, drama and movement. These can, collectively (or individually) be delivered with careful consideration into most home gardens.

3 As it flows down the inside of this curved wall, the water gives a sense of movement and shine to the black timber. It then levels out to form a shallow lap pool.

Simple and effective water

When most people think of including water in their home garden, an image of a small, natural-looking pond or off-the-shelf water feature is conjured up. However, these features never really produce the often-required need for reflection, views or drama. Introducing still water into a garden can be a daunting task, but with confidence and an eye for detail it can be dramatic and significant.

Done really well it can set the whole tone of the outside space. The materials and shape can reflect any style of design, but consideration must also be given to its scale, maintenance requirements, topographical demands, the safety for garden users and its possible attraction to household pets. Once these are answered, flat water can then become an integral part of a great garden design.

2

STILL WATERS SOMETIMES RUN DEEP

Even though some of these creations are for show gardens, their principles can easily be applied to a home garden.

1 This expanse of seemingly bottomless water acts like a blank sheet dividing lawn from building. Note the ingenious square shafts where the water falls over the edge and down into the void below – a great piece of design.

2 Using water to complement other materials is a clever trick: here, simple rectangles of still water continue the linear grid of this space, softened by dense planting on the outside edges. Deck walkways seemingly hover above the water at right angles.

3 Water acts like a sheen over these beautiful sculptures, and in so doing shows how it can enhance another garden feature.

4 This long thin mini-canal directs the visitor's eye to the orangery at the far end – a traditional design technique in formal and often grand gardens.

3

4

DEFINED ROLE

Water can often be used successfully in a complementary, low-key way; it doesn't always have to be the main focus of a design.

1 The blue glass sculpture is the centre of attention here, while the water at its base plays second fiddle but helps 'anchor' the sculpture into the scene.

2 Movement, texture and simplicity are all entwined in this creation; there is writing beneath the water's surface, while the step down reinforces the sense of movement.

3 This mirror-polished steel sculptural form, surrounded by lush, green ferns, makes a huge statement of high-quality design in this garden's cool corner.

4 A holed-out stone provides a perfect balance to the informal planting and rustic fence, and is easily replicated in a home garden. Such simplicity can be highly effective.

5 Rusting steel troughs seem to slice through the raised tree canopy above and frothy planting below. Their successful positioning exemplifies how important it is to consider how any container will sit within its surroundings.

6 The subtle addition of water hawthorn (*Aponogeton distachyos*) in this over-sized container brings colour to the flat surface, and gives interest to the overall effect.

EXPERT TIP
Andrew Ewing Edging water

‶The use of an appropriate material around your water feature can substantially enhance its overall design and effect. For a minimal edging, say, between grass and water, stainless steel set upright produces a crisp line and can allow the water height to be almost level with the grass. Otherwise stone is a great edging material, whether cut clean in a modern style or left more naturalistic and jagged. When using stone it always helps to have an overhang at the side of the pool, to create an elegant line and to help conceal any pond lining. Other materials can of course be used, but they raise very real and practical concerns of load bearing (that is, how much weight that material can take when stood on) and fixing (if there is an overhang over the water, how do you ensure that standing on the overhang won't make the visitor topple into the water). Consider also wildlife needs, in terms of how amphibians may enter or exit the water, and also the role and requirements of aquatic and marginal planting if desired. Such planting can 'soften' the edge of a water feature, directing attention onto the plants and water itself.〞

[above] How you edge a water feature – and what material you choose – are crucial in helping set the overall tone of a design.

[right] A more naturalistic approach to edging a pond here uses *Sarracenia* arising out of 'black' water, with a timber deck beyond. Note the *Sarracenia* would not be hardy in cool-temperate regions.

ACHIEVING A NATURAL FEEL

Informal planting, irregular edges and rustic materials can combine to create a strong effect.

1 This pond adds to the overall feel of a naturally inspired garden by looking as if it has been here for many years, The effect is made all the more convincing by marginal planting, rocks and plenty of algae.

2 A small detail, such as a white-flowering *Iris*, comfortably growing in the lee of this rock, makes for a realistic touch.

3 Water flows through a main pond, flanked by shallow overflow pools, in this recreation of a cottage-style garden. The materials and design were chosen to cope with flash flooding and sporadic heavy rainfall.

4 Chelsea pensioners add to this quintessentially British scene of a derelict fence tumbling into an informal water area. Dressed in their famous red coats, the pensioners are an intrinsic part of the show, which is held at the grounds of the Royal Hospital Chelsea.

Soft planting within and around water can be quite a challenge. The cerise-pink of candelabra primulas and round-leaved hostas soften the edge of the raised water feature and visually tie in with the French lavender in the foreground.

The Real Rubbish Garden, Claire Whitehouse, 2005

Movement in all shapes and sizes

Gardeners and designers often want water features to be visually useful as well as dynamic and interesting. One way of contributing to such a goal is to make the water move – whether a slow trickle or full-on jet. Either way, moving water can not only look incredibly attractive and dramatic – no matter what the style – but it can also ensure oxygen is introduced to the water, which in turns helps reduce stagnation. If creating a feature with moving water, however, beware that substantial disturbance may upset wildlife and some plants, so consider the type of motion needed for the effect desired. Also understand how the movement is to be created (pump? gravity?) and if it will require additional technical knowledge. Water can be a difficult material to make work well, so research and predict what problems may arise before getting the spade out and making your dream creation.

FORM AND STYLE FOR ANY GARDEN

Making water move can be achieved in myriad ways, from shoots or waterfalls to containers or jets.

1 This simple linear feature lets the water fall into a trough below, and at night it is accentuated by the addition of a bright white-red light.

2 A water jet 'leaping' over the planting onto the wall beyond brings a sense of the unexpected to a small urban space. Such an element of surprise can be a real novelty in a garden.

3 Misting machines can be used to add an air of mystery or drama to water, but the context and the surrounding materials are crucial to make sure the rising mist looks convincing.

4 This glass sculpture, by light sculptor Iestyn Davies, features oil and air, swirling and mixing around to great effect; colour-changing LED lights accentuate the drama at night.

5 On this back 'wall', water drips from one slat to another, accentuating the natural curve and using water to bring added movement. By merging structure, sculpture and water feature all into one, the designer has created a work of art in itself.

6 Waterfalls, when done well, can be a great way to hide an unsightly wall, unwanted view or block out noise. As here, ensure the drop of each water layer is well positioned and physically relates to those above or below.

7 This swirling vortex is an interesting detail within a much larger expanse of otherwise still water.

JETS FOR VERTICAL FORM

By making water rise vertically, in the form of a spray or jet, movement and energy can be introduced into a design.

1 This simple spray of water can be included in any domestic water feature; ensure surrounding planting is moisture-tolerant as wind can blow water in different directions.

2 Low 'bubbles' help move the body of water over the raised plinth edge to the basin below. Blending such simplicity with highly skilled construction techniques can be quite challenging, but the end result, as here, is well worth it.

3 Spiralling glass pebbles around the outside of the feature accentuate the strong thick jet. Their placement adds movement, and the white froth of the water creates a sense of energy.

4 The combination of square pool, vertical jet, double layer box hedge and wide steps makes for a simply stunning formal scheme that is both refined and proportionally exact.

[right] These simple cubes of water with their flat surfaces reflect the sky and light from above, and contrast in tone and texture with the plants around them.

[far right] A great sculptured white 'ball' here seems to be sending out ripples of water from its epicentre as well as subtly mirroring the sky and trees.

EXPERT TIP
Andrew Ewing Reflections

❝ The basic principle of creating reflections is to use a dark material as a liner for the pool. If you envisage a puddle on black Tarmac you can understand this; although the puddle may be only a couple of centimetres deep, it can create a perfect mirror image. The lining material in the pool is not important, but its colouring is. For a sharp reflection, the water needs to appear as still as possible, with no debris disturbing the surface. This can be a problem in small urban gardens (with leaves or pollen falling onto the

4

surface) but if you can plan the location of the water feature in the most open area of your plot, that is ideal. Ensuring the water feature is also built level is crucial, because the water surface will be unforgiving if there is even a slight camber. Remember, however, that even though reflections are amazing for many water features, on overcast and dull days the effect can be diminished, so be sure you choose the style and shape of your water feature correctly. Lighting can also be considered in tandem with the use of reflections: think about highlighting the feature to be mirrored in the water, not the water itself, so for example illuminate a tree that will be reflected in the water. The end result can be a really subtle but stunning way to link the night-time atmosphere of planting with the water in your garden. '

DROPS FOR DRAMA

A sheer drop or a more subtle 'stepped' effect can each set the overall tone of a water feature to great effect.

1 This sheer wall is a magnificent creation – especially as the reclining incline is subtle, offset beautifully by the surrounding yew hedge, and simple gravel strip at its base; at night, the spotlights create even more drama.

2 A rusticated rock wall artfully mimics the sense of energy and movement one might expect with a natural waterfall. The placement of submerged lights adds to the feeling of water plunging into a deep pool below. The white allium flowerheads in the foreground are also well set off by the water.

3 Simple droplets of water fall from one slat to the next, helping create a semitransparent screen.

4 This 'wall' of water cascades from a thick metal top bar, to produce a moving, changeable and unusual feature.

5 Precision-perfect flat water, defined level changes and varying pace combine to sublime effect. Many elements (sculpture, water, planting, movement) were brought together in this scheme, which sought to represent the flow of New Zealand water from mountain streams down to the sea.

This seamless piece of design brings the simplicity of the water feature up against the natural beauty of form and colour (the mixed planting). Together they provide a garden view that is bold, confident and contemporary, but has warmth and depth to it.
The Halifax Garden 'These Four Walls', Stuart Perry, 2006

5

6

FOCUSING WATER'S DIRECTION

There are many ways in which water can be channelled, and these can vary from bold statements to simple effects.

1 This stainless steel water arc provides an entrance to the garden, while the swirling mosaic (created by Maggy Howarth) continues the aquatic theme.

2 A contemporary glass sculpture channels the movement of water in a specific direction. Speed of flow and cleanliness of water are essential in helping this design succeed.

3 Water from a slot in the wall drops into the basin below. Such a simple detail could be introduced to enliven the corner of a wall in any home garden.

4 The subtle use of water here has created interest and given sound to an area of garden yet without demanding too much attention.

5 This clever scheme uses two overflowing, York-stone trays to allow water to pass down to a waist-level pool; and then another tray lets this water feed into the large rill below.

6 A small water chute cleverly mirrors the size of the wooden cubes, while water from its outflow forms random paths down the steps.

7 Three lacquered-steel bespoke water features project out of this wall – their shape was inspired by an arum lily.

7

THE DAILY TELEGRAPH GARDEN

Having the confidence to fill much of your allocated space at the RHS Chelsea Flower Show with water requires real conviction. In this garden, Arabella Lennox-Boyd showed how water can play equal fiddle to inanimate objects, such as stones or paving, and to ever-changing subjects such as plants and trees. Her pared-down space used quality materials rather than garden-gizmos to show what can be achieved when Japanese design principles are combined with English planting.

Often at Chelsea, gardens are created on the assumption that what is on display would actually make up only part of a larger garden, if it were ever to enter 'the real world'. With this in mind, it is easy to start to appreciate this design more and more. A large rectangle of water takes up nearly three-quarters of the space, yet the designer's intention to 'simply provide delight and to create an atmosphere of peace and relaxation' cannot be refuted.

WHY THIS GARDEN WORKS SO WELL:
- the water area is crossed by two ribbons of differing materials – one of waterlily *Nymphaea alba* and the other of a Burlington-slate path;
- the sinuous lines of these ribbons converge and retreat, so they are visually balanced by two large slate rocks;
- the visitor's eye is then lifted to the planting: along one edge a clipped tiered yew hedge, and then at the end is an area of dense planting consisting of greens, whites, beige/yellows and textured bark and stems;
- the mirror-like qualities of the water reflect nearby and far-off views;
- the detailing, whether slate mulch surrounding the water or the stones that emerge from it, is pin sharp and very clean;
- a hidden mirror behind the bamboo stems at the far end gives extra depth and light to the whole space.

So what about home gardens? This design tells you everything you need to know about water: why levels are so important; how to use materials that will visually link across a scheme; and the reflective quality that only water can bring and how best to use it. It also gives neat ideas: that of balancing dense planting (a mass) with the air above the water (a void); of simple-to-achieve lines (the water's edge, yew hedge and so on) that hold the space and take the garden visitor from one space to another; and of harmonious planting in terms of flower and leaf colour.

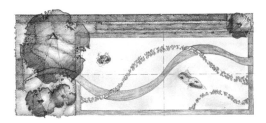

And don't forget the mirror behind the bamboo – a great trick that anyone can achieve, as long as you remember to hide the mirror's edges with dense planting so you can't see where the mirror starts and ends.

DESIGNER Arabella Lennox-Boyd

CONTRACTOR Crocus.co.uk

AWARD Gold

CATEGORY Show Garden, 2008

SPONSOR *The Daily Telegraph*

KEY WORDS water; path; green-and-white planting; bamboo stems; reflection; waterlilies

IN A SENTENCE... A calming balancing act between planting, water and stone.

1 *Pterocarya fraxinifolia* – a vigorous, spreading tree that likes to grow in deep, fertile, moist but well-drained soil – visually offsets the flat calm water and gives height to the space. Its ovate, glossy green leaves contrast nicely with the slender form of the neighbouring *Phyllostachys* bamboo.

2 *Gunnera manicata*, a large-leaved, waterside-loving plant, creates a strong focal point at the end of the garden, contrasting in both texture and shape with the yew hedge to the right, and sleek paving below.

3 This slate path brings movement and curves to the rectangular water area, which it divides. The sweep of the path is cleverly mirrored by sinuous plantings of white waterlily – an ingenious way of using different materials while retaining a consistent design effect.

4 Tall rocks within a water feature should be considered in terms of how and where most visitors will view the design. This will provoke the strongest 'wow' factor.

5 The expanse of water contributes greatly to the success of this garden, as do the subsequent reflections that are created not only of the surrounding trees of *Platanus* x *hispanica* or the focal-point bamboos, but also of the clouds and pockets of white sky.

6 Waterlilies *Nymphaea alba*, planted in two opposing curves, form part of the floral splendour of this garden, which comes from the restrained palette of plants used and their subsequent flower colour – purely white.

THE CHRIS BEARDSHAW GARDEN – 'GROWING FOR LIFE' AT BOVERIDGE HOUSE

In some schemes, water can be a dominant feature, staking a claim for the overall 'wow factor' of a garden. But here, in this exquisitely detailed garden by Chris Beardshaw, water acts as a leveller, giving symmetry and formality to the space, allowing plants and garden elements to shine. The area of the water, its shape in relation to the surrounding paving, and the inclusion of a water fountain and waterlilies, formed a cohesive, convincing style. This was a scheme that is easy to copy at home, and one that gave a sentimental and recognisable feeling of history, a sense of English countryside and country house style.

In essence, this was a simple garden – one applicable to any long narrow strip of land. Its ingredients, too, were uncomplicated: rectangular water feature, stone paving, dense planting, clipped hedging, pots and garden ornaments, and a focal point of a stone gazebo/loggia. However, it was their combination and creation that showed true skill. The design was based on a garden at Boveridge House, Dorset, where landscape architect Thomas Mawson and garden designer Gertrude Jekyll created a quintessentially English garden in the 1920s.

SO WHAT WORKS SO WELL IN THIS GARDEN?
- the pond runs the length of the planting bed, and takes the visitor's eye down to the loggia;
- the waterlilies break up the flat surface of the water and the rectangular edges of the paving, adding colour (leaves and flowers) to the water;
- the planting in the main borders is dense. In a real garden this would need careful management – so one plant didn't outcompete the other – but the effect can be recreated with sensible plant choices and an understanding of growth requirements;
- the selection of flower colour and shape give a traditionally British feel, with an air of romance and slight haphazardness;
- 'supporting' elements such as a cherub-like, trickling water feature, planted pots and an old-fashioned wheelbarrow add to the effect.

Even though most people don't have a country house with which to support this garden, its design and creation are applicable to any place. It may look simple, but the reason this recreation is so convincing is because of its use of focal point (looking down towards the gazebo), balanced proportion (area of pond to area of paving to area of planting), appropriate scale (planting gradually increasing in height the further away from the pond) and colour harmony (flowers, leaves, stonework, pots and so on).

Designer Chris Beardshaw

CONTRACTOR Peter Dowle Plants and Gardens

AWARD Gold

CATEGORY Show Garden, 2006

KEY WORDS balanced; traditional; formal; dense planting; waterlilies; country house; country garden; garden building

IN A SENTENCE... Elegant reproduction of a traditional but tasteful design.

1 Purple leaved copper beech (*Fagus sylvatica Atropurpurea* Group) provides a feeling of maturity and visual interest. The trees behind give the same effect as in many domestic gardens – by visually 'borrowing' your neighbour's plants, you give the impression that your garden is bigger than it actually is.

2 This stone loggia, overlooking the long water feature and beautiful planting, is crying out to be sat in. Not many other gardens could support such a beautiful building.

3 The mixture of tall foxgloves (*Digitalis*), red roses and tiered *Viburnum plicatum* f. *tomentosum* 'Mariesii', in these densely planted borders either side of the water feature, offer a timeless feel; but beware: such dense planting would not be sustainable in most domestic-sized gardens.

4 An old-fashioned wheelbarrow adding to a sense of age, as well as some spring-flowering pots, give the impression that this is a real and working garden, which is no exception to the idea that Chelsea gardens require a bit of theatre design.

5 The water level is slightly lower than the surrounding paving, so a sense of depth is created. In addition, by including a relatively dense canopy of waterlilies, the designer is helping give the impression that this is a mature established garden – a useful trick if you desire to make your garden more instant.

MATERIALS

Whether a brand-new material
or an older material used in
a contemporary and different
way, the endless creativity
on display at Chelsea is utterly
breathtaking.

One thing that Chelsea designers really enjoy is being able to experiment with new materials. It gives these creative people the opportunity to try out some new techniques or products that their working life may not afford them. No real clients, no real restrictions; no real issues of taste and no practical problems of longevity or weather – this show lets them break rules and push tried-and-tested boundaries.

1

Garden and landscape designers are often reputed to have quite a lonely existence in their working lives. Of course, they see their clients and suppliers, but much of the time is spent on their own, devising designs, creating planting plans and sourcing products. Yet by nature most are creative, design-aware people who enjoy the stimulation of working with others and challenging artisans – from sculptors to builders, carpenters to quarrymen – to transform their ideas into reality. The ever-expanding exchange of information and ideas from architects, interior designers, sculptors and product designers is increasingly leading to a healthy development of visual and conceptual exploration. Sharing ideas, learning from other trades and researching other professions all feed an appetite for new concepts. RHS Chelsea Flower Show is, in a way, the end of that process for many designers as it is a forum where they can showcase the results of this development process. But for the gardening public, it may be just the start.

So what type of materials are being shown at Chelsea? In short, any. During recent years, more glass has been used outside, as a direct result of advancements in specification and manufacturing. Whether as screens or balustrades, tables or water sculptures, glass can be an expensive yet splendid addition to a show garden. So too can metal – from stainless steel planters to rusting steel, the diversity of finishes to, and types of, metal can provide endless opportunity for designers. The form in which metal has often been included varies from the rustic to the contemporary, low-key to the overt, bespoke to off-the-shelf items. Perspex, normally attributed to indoor products, has also been used in some show gardens in recent years, as developments in its formation – plus the realisation that it can bring colour and a variety of shapes to a garden – have been welcomed by those wanting a statement feature. As well as these man-made materials, long-appreciated timber never fails to whet designer's appetites, either in fantastic sculptural additions (see case study, p150) or in much smaller interventions of seating or tables.

Much of what is seen at Chelsea can trigger the reaction 'I want one of those' – even by the most restrained of gardeners. However what is on display in a show garden may be completely new to the garden world, so its longevity, its ability to cope with years of changeable weather conditions, and its actual structural rigidity are not necessarily proven. It may be a designer's chance to try out a technique or concept as yet unseen – something that may look visually stunning but actually needs further refinement. This doesn't mean that you shouldn't get excited when you see a material used in a completely different way, but it may be best to temper your enthusiasm by considering just how well that material would work in a real, 365-days-a-year garden.

The upshot of all this design novelty is often to be seen in the garden centres and DIY shops a few years later. Just like the catwalk of the fashion world, techniques and products on

1 Using materials from unexpected sources can be personally rewarding and environmentally friendly. Here the designer has included offcuts of wood – by-products from the timber industry – to create a decorative and textured wall. The variation in colour and the way that the wood has been laid at varying indentations make for a great effect.

2 A concoction of architectural planting, unusual paving, strongly coloured walls and bold planters can work well together, provided there is a clear vision of what aesthetic outcome is desired.

3 Drama can be created using a range of clever design principles. Here the combination of three primary materials – steel, stone and timber – contrast yet complement each other (see case study, p100).

4 The 'magic' of different materials can be exploited by their application as much as by their inherent form. The different lines – here of a bench and retaining wall, softened by colourful planting – make for a visual treat.

display at Chelsea sometimes end up (sometimes pared down) in the home environment. Consider the fire pit, for example: a simple device, either dug into the ground or standing proud (similar to a mini-barbecue) that allows you to burn wood in your garden, in a safe and attractive way. Seen at Chelsea in different guises over the years, it is now a common item among some of the more contemporary product lines in fashionable garden-related shops.

Fortunately, the net result for all garden consumers is an expansion of choice and range of styles, whether these act as an aesthetic stimulation that sparks an interest in the viewer, or a few years later they result in a product that has been developed for the mass market. For some visitors, Chelsea show gardens provide the encouragement to recreate the same designs at home; for others, they supply the source for an appropriate artisan or manufacturer to fulfil their immediate needs. What is certain is that the material magic of Chelsea show gardens will continue to challenge and stimulate the creative minds of designers and gardeners alike.

Metal in many guises

The advent of more refined manufacturing techniques, plus the ever-expanding thirst of designers for novelty, have brought a host of new ideas on how to use different metals in a garden setting at the RHS Chelsea Flower Show. From planters to dividing screens, planting edges to garden sculptures, the practical and visual appeal of metal is integral to many show gardens. One such example has been the popular use of gabions (metal cages filled with stone, soil or any other material) that derive from the civil engineering industry, and are intended to retain landform behind. Their application in show gardens has brought a whole new suite of ideas fresh from designers.

But it is perhaps the variety of end results that makes using metal so interesting. Whether it is stainless steel or galvanised, brushed or polished, steel especially has brought new opportunities for designers both as the primary material on show and in a supporting role. And, as is often the case with Chelsea ideas, similar ideas and styles are now percolating through the supply chain into garden centres, DIY stores or through online shops.

3

ANY SHAPE WILL DO

From gabions to sculpture, planters to water features, metal engineering can be introduced in a range of ways.

1 This repetitively shaped planter is a great addition to any wall or small space, providing vertical interest to a garden. Each individual unit – here growing pansies – gives just enough planting depth for a seasonal display.

2 A simple cylindrical design evokes a futuristic feel in this space. The smooth metallic surface complements beautifully the weeping habit of this cactus.

3 Soda-blasted aluminium 'thought bubbles' have been designed to link with the sponsor's message. Their inclusion nicely balances the green wall behind, contrasting in both form and colour with the foreground planting and clean linear steps.

4 Where gabions are used in a garden setting, the engineering requirement may be reduced, while the aesthetic benefit they bring is truly maximised.

5 By combining water and steel a dramatic impression can be created in a garden, as can be seen here, where water is flowing down the sides of these sculptural features.

4

5

Materials up close

One of the great challenges of working with a range of materials is understanding how they look when viewed in close proximity, as this may be very different to the splendour and drama a material may convey when seen from a distance. Designers therefore take great care in ensuring any creation looks as good up close as it does from afar. In a home garden this rule is even more important, as the materials used will be seen most days, and in a range of different weathers and light conditions. When considering how materials look up close, remember that their construction and finish can really help convey a quality feel to the scheme.

3

ALL IN THE DETAIL

When putting materials together, consider the relationship they have in terms of colour, form and texture.

1 A wall of Western Australian sandstone brings colour and texture to this area, demanding closer inspection of the material itself, as well as its quality construction.

2 The rammed earth wall provides a striking backdrop to the bold planting of palms, succulents and cacti. The strong coppery-orange and grey-black striated colours link to the garden's theme of an astronaut's tour of duty on the planet Mars.

3 This play garden included a variety of materials – plastic piping, natural stone paving, succulent and herbaceous planting – all in close succession, but to good effect. The stone is the end of a snake's tail.

EXPERT TIP
Andy Sturgeon Decking

❛ Essentially there are three types of decking for gardens:

- Tropical hardwood is the most expensive material and undoubtedly looks the most sophisticated. It is also the longest lasting timber and as decking should endure for as much as 40–60 years. Apart from their initial colours, there is little to choose between the various types, which have exotic names like Ipe and Balau, although in time sunlight will turn all of them the same silvery grey.
- Pressure-treated softwood will last less than half as long as tropical hardwood but is considerably cheaper to buy. It is easier to cut and drill, so quicker to install.
- Western red cedar falls somewhere between the other two in terms of looks, quality, price and workability.

Lay boards 'smooth side up' for a superior look, especially as the grooves in decking trap dirt and can become slippery. Pressure wash decking at least once a year. Secure decking with 'lost head' screws, which 'disappear' into the wood and don't become unwanted visual features.

Hardwoods and cedar do not need preservatives; any silvering can be removed (if required) with chemicals or pressure washing and oils, and then be restored or retained by applying appropriately tinted products. Preservatives and stains can prolong the life of softwood and improve its appearance, but avoid using varnishes because they flake and peel. ❜

Decking continues to be a popular choice with gardeners, making the outside space, weather permitting, useable throughout the year.

1

2

Just add timber

Wood is probably the most versatile of garden materials. Not only does it have a huge emotional attraction for many gardeners (who doesn't love to stand against a mighty oak or stroke an unusual bark?), but it can also be made into seats, fences, steps, structures, screens or surfaces. Timber is timeless and can be used to great effect – in a modern or traditional, formal or naturalistic way. Its finishes too are endless, with stains, paints, effects and quality providing huge possibilities, as demonstrated so successfully by designers in the RHS Chelsea Flower Show gardens. There, the ability of craftspeople to sculpt and transform a piece of wood from a designer's concept into an actual reality can be fully appreciated. And it is this combining of skills – designer vision with technical ability – that is at the heart of so many gardening successes throughout the world.

3

4

TIMBER IN DIFFERENT GUISES

Working with timber can be enjoyable in any garden, whether you
are an enthusiastic amateur or skilled carpenter.

1 To break up the linear effect of this decking, chamomile has been
planted across the timber lines. The 'squiggle' effect makes for a really
interesting contrast, allowing planting and wood to balance each other.

2 First-grade Western red cedar has been used in this scheme. It is
a timber full of natural resins which make it highly durable – and not
necessary to stain. As the wood naturally weathers, it will become a
more silver colour. The cantilevered bench makes good use of space.

3 Seemingly random cubes of oak rise at different heights from the
black water below, acting as a flight of steps. The aquatic and marginal
planting softens the overall effect, and the result is a great example of
material combination.

4 Decking is an ever-popular flooring material for both professional
and home gardeners, but the addition of different materials – such as
the steel mesh here – can make the result more visually exciting.

5 To partition this space, the designer placed the perforated timber
'walls' at a slight diagonal across the garden. The silver-grey paint
references the colour used on many buildings in the Swedish
countryside (linking to the design theme).

5

Full on colour

While well-planned planting selections can bring foliage and floral colour to most gardens, inanimate objects can really help add a blast of much-needed vibrancy. Containers or planters can be used to provide a strong block of colour, while paving can be designed so there is a consistent 'flow' of tonal texture in a space. More dramatic additions can be verging on the sculptural, with mosaics or surface treatments bringing a whole new range of hues and shades to an otherwise ordinary garden. Before using colour so boldly, however, there are two important considerations: make sure you really like the colours you are including (as the novelty value can soon wear off); and remember that strong vivid colours can look somewhat ungainly or out-of-place under overcast grey skies. Once you have resolved these issues, colour can be welcomed with great enthusiasm.

SPECTRUM OF CHOICE

A host of materials from glass to stone, metal to timber can be introduced to expand the colour range in a garden.

1 This dramatic container creates a definite focal point – the swirling mosaic design on the outside is continued within, in the form of a sculptural plant. Note how the colours are carried on at ground level with red and yellow bedding plants.

2 The detail and intricacy of a design such as this mosaic path is not for the faint hearted, and must be undertaken by a skilled artisan for best effect.

3 Representing cracked and melting ice – the designer's response to recent changes in the climate – this water wall provides a startling backdrop to the more low-key planting at its base.

4 Colours, textures, shapes and styles abound in this view, from the traditional deckchairs on the roof of the garden room to the stone-filled gabions, with masses of dense and colourful planting in the foreground. This accumulation of colour makes for a bold and flamboyant effect.

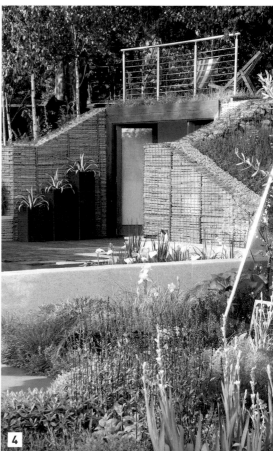

3

4

Bringing the space alive

Screens, walls, fences and hedges are popular design elements used in all types of gardens (see also pp32–7). Their use can be practical (to define a certain area of planting or give climatic protection) or it can be physical (to make a space feel bigger or a certain area more intimate). Yet the material that they are constructed from can help set the whole tone of the garden. The colour can inject excitement or calm; the texture can be rough, smooth, metallic or matt; the size can be proportionate, overdominant or undersized; and the material itself can clash or complement. Whatever materials or techniques you use for delineating your garden, ensure that they can withstand the vagaries of the weather, can be maintained to the standard required, and will mature and develop as intended.

DIVIDING SPACE

A range of techniques can be adopted to make a space feel bigger.

1 Orange Perspex screens help give depth and interest to this space. Note how the colour of the screens links to the orange-red tulips, while the burgundy-leaved *Dahlia* adds a darker tone.

2 Undulating grass paths in this scheme create movement and flow, and help trick the visitor's eye into thinking the space is bigger than it is. Smooth painted render on the side walls enhance the effect.

3 An image of botanist, scientist and explorer Carl Linnaeus has been imprinted on a vertical, laser-cut sheet of steel in this garden so he seemingly overlooks the space. The screen also breaks up the view of the white-flowering foxgloves and hedge beyond.

EXPERT TIP
Andy Sturgeon Using glass

' Glass is useful in the garden for furniture, screens, balustrades and flooring but is quite a specialist material that often needs expert installation. Generally speaking it should be toughened for safety and should not have sharp corners at adult or child head height. Clear glass requires regular cleaning as it readily shows the dirt; opaque, coloured or patterned glass perhaps less so. Acrylic/Perspex/Plexiglass (it's all the same material) is lighter and less expensive than glass, making it a better choice for roof gardens and balconies, and for gardens where access is difficult. It is far more versatile, easier to cut, polish and glue and readily available in a wide range of colours and therefore suitable for anything from planters to water features and clever lighting features. Ultraviolet and impact-resistant acrylics are available but being quite flexible they are less able to take loads than glass, making them unsuitable for flooring or balustrades. Avoid abrasive cleaning products on acrylics. '

While allowing light to filter in, these glass panels help divide this small space into a path on the left and a planting area to the right.

The overriding beauty of this scheme is the contrast of the linear expanse of timber and knapped flint with the planting. The cedar deck is oiled to enhance its colour and grey paving, metal kickboards and grey-black flint balance the vision.

The Savills Garden, Marcus Barnett and Philip Nixon, 2007

1

Thinking outside the box

Some of the most innovative, aesthetic designs sometimes stem from combining materials that are not normally seen together. Putting rough with the smooth, the bright with the plain or the textured with the matt is fun but challenging. To mix materials skilfully you need an understanding of their similarities as well as their differences. Should you be contrasting form with texture, or practicality with visual drama? Can one material embellish another, or should both be equal partners?

How can one material physically juxtapose another, especially when both materials may require different construction techniques? When done badly, some material combinations can look a mess; by looking tacky the final effect can unintentionally destroy the original thoughts behind them. When done well, on the other hand, they can be creative, stimulating and a fresh way of viewing materials.

DIFFERENT MATERIALS, DIFFERENT IDEAS

Mixing materials takes skill and effort, but when done well the results can be really exciting.

1 These terracotta- and stone-filled gabions not only provide a sustainable response by using reclaimed or old materials, but also act as a low retaining wall to the planting behind. The additional benefit for insects to nest or house within the gaps is considerable.

2 Handcrafted zinc tanks feature throughout this garden, the still black water complementing the silver-grey of the zinc container (see case study, p78). Such simplicity in material juxtaposition can create sublime detailing.

3 These striking mature cacti look fabulous within the black planter, with a black wall behind creating a cool calm atmosphere. The white mulch also heightens the sense of modernity.

4 Designers are not allowed to include current models of cars in gardens, as this could be deemed advertising, but here a crushed car has been recycled to help form an outdoor table. Surrounded by clean, modern lines, the contrast of texture and colour is a great success.

5 The concept for this space was an outside gallery, displaying a private collection of photographs. The metallic side panels, framed photographs and rendered wall combine to strong effect.

IN THE GROVE

There are some designers whose style is so identifiable that their trademark is their very essence. Christopher Bradley-Hole is one such designer: his gardens have a highly restrained feeling, coupled with a completeness and sense of calm that when you view them you know that every bit of space has been thought through, changed, questioned, revised and agreed upon. In addition, he uses both new and old materials to great effect. For gardeners, his work shows that by really thinking through the detail as well as the overall design a high-quality garden can be created, wherever the location and whatever the budget.

This garden used horizontals and verticals to the maximum. The design was based on the notion of a grove as a 'mythical and intellectual place in historic gardens' but with a minimalist, contemporary interpretation. The result was a calming and private space, dappled with light and textural interest. The choice of materials was relatively simple – bamboos, yew hedging, boardwalk, stone walls, planting and stone mulch – yet their execution and combination resulted in a garden full of interest but with an underlying cohesion. And it is this that is probably most important to consider: a unity of materials and colours is a vital way of bringing a space together. You have to be certain that the materials you have chosen work well in close proximity and are ones you really like. If they are, then the end result can look, like here, truly superb.

OTHER ELEMENTS TO NOTE FROM THIS GARDEN:

- tall bamboos give height, colour (the vivid jade-green canes in particular) and cast shadows below; they also manage to add a lightness to the overall feel;
- yew hedging divides the space, but is kept quite low (to about 1m/3ft) so that when the garden visitor walks through the garden the views are maintained, but when sitting down privacy is created;
- a diagonal timber boardwalk gives visual continuity running along the length of the garden and connects two stone terraces;
- flower and plant choice is selective, with peonies, grasses and perennials mixing to strong effect.

DESIGNER Christopher Bradley-Hole

CONTRACTOR Steven Swatton

AWARD Gold

CATEGORY Show Garden, 2005

SPONSOR His late Highness Shaikh Zayed bin Sultan Al-Nahyan

KEY WORDS restrained; calm; cool; minimalist; confident; high-quality; considered

IN A SENTENCE... A restrained and contemporary garden that oozes quality and reinforces modernist principles in a refreshing way.

1 Tall bamboo (*Phyllostachys iridescens*) lends a strong vertical element to the garden, making it feel much bigger than it really is. Note how the leaves and branches have been removed from the culms (canes) to about shoulder height, allowing air into the garden and making a feature of their beautiful colour.

2 Light-coloured limestone walls have been used as a backdrop. Their effect is not only to lighten the whole space but also to heighten visual interest, by using horizontal lines to accentuate the garden's length and breadth. The linear design of the walls also links nicely with the timber deck.

3 Yew (*Taxus baccata*) hedging has been kept low (growing to about 1m/3ft tall), giving a frame to the surrounding planting, emphasising the linear nature of the space, and bringing a deep green colour and solid mass to the garden. The hedges also create discrete areas in themselves, establishing more intimate areas of interest.

4 These red peonies add a deep colour as well as a tonal link to the timber walk; white peonies lighten the area beyond and link to the limestone walls. Although floral colour is limited in this garden, what has been chosen has been used for good reason.

5 This cube stone mulch is a truly lovely way of bringing varying colours and tones to the ground plan, each cube a thing of beauty. Chelsea is well known for bringing such new ideas to public attention.

6 Timber decking has had a bad press, mainly through overuse, bad choice of stain and misuse of protected wood. Here, however, the specification and use are spot-on: a diagonal layout provides movement through the space, the construction is immaculate, with invisible fixings, and the colour adds to the overall feel.

CANCER RESEARCH UK GARDEN

Every few years at Chelsea one of the show gardens features an iconic statement that is not only memorable for itself but also sums up the whole show. In 2007, garden designer Andy Sturgeon created just such a stir. His Cancer Research UK garden represented just how far sculpture and garden could combine: how the physical properties of a man-made oak structure, 30m (100ft) long, could seamlessly 'swim' through the air, as well as in and out of plants. It represented a symbiotic relationship of structure and flora seemingly living, moving and breathing together. Rarely has Chelsea seen such a combination work so successfully, while at the same time so strongly supporting the sponsor's message of 'together we will beat cancer'.

The designer is well known for creating modern, contemporary, highly styled gardens, mainly for well-off clients in the southeast of the UK and abroad. But he always manages to balance planting with hard materials. He adopts a similar approach for his show gardens, which are often jam-packed with plants, sublime construction and usually offset with some statement effect – maybe sculpture, a building or ingenious level changes. For many gardeners, his designs may seem unrealistic – in both budget and style – but look beyond the showmanship and you can see some really strong design working incredibly hard. There is much of this approach that can be transcribed to your back garden.

ELEMENTS THAT MIGHT BE USED IN A DOMESTIC SETTING:

- the combinations of plant shape, texture and colour, with each other and other built forms (sculpture, paving or building), creates interest, contrast and seasonal differentiation;
- by fully including such an incredible piece of sculpture from the outset, the planting and location of all the other elements within the space can be worked out;
- the delineation of areas by simple yew hedging brings a sense of formality and consistency across the space and also engenders a sense of visual respite from the rest of the planting;
- optimum use of space, which is vital for gardeners; here a linear path takes the visitor to a Japanese-inspired pavilion for contemplation and looking out across the garden.

The garden seemingly moves, changes and swirls before your eyes, but if you take a closer look you can see that this space invites you to experience it. For most people, that is what a garden should do.

1 Hedging has been used at different levels (from waist height to shoulder height) to subdivide the space, while also acting as a simple green backdrop for the diverse range of plants at ground level.

2 This Portugese limestone path acts to 'calm' the space down and provides a feeling of light and respite from the textural and colour combinations elsewhere. With gardens that have many elements within them, such as this, it is often best to keep paths simple.

DESIGNER Andy Sturgeon

CONTRACTOR The Outdoor Room

AWARD Gold

CATEGORY Show Garden, 2007

SPONSOR Cancer Research

KEY WORDS oak sculpture; dense planting; texture; outdoor pavilion; contemporary; movement; flow

IN A SENTENCE... This sublime garden mixes colour, texture and shape to great effect, bringing hard and soft materials seamlessly together.

3 This oak sculpture, 30m (100ft) long, twists and entwines with itself and the planting below. Such a sculpture would cost a substantial part of a home garden budget (and would need more rigorous support), but its level of spectacle should inspire most creative gardeners. It was probably one of the most striking features of recent Chelseas.

4 An open-sided pavilion provides a place to relax – crucial for most gardeners. The black frames allow the structure to merge into the background, while the yellow chairs (created by Italian designer Paola Lenti with woven yachting rope) add a dash of vivid colour – here nicely offset by the dark yew hedges.

5 Different leaf form and colour – most notably, silver-leaved cardoons – have been used to maintain interest at ground level. Note, though, that in a real garden and after a summer's growth the plants will be nearer to head height so there will be quite a different feel to this space.

6 A beautiful *Cornus controversa* tree anchors the space, growing taller than the sculpture but with an airiness that allows light and sight into the garden. In successful gardens, the vertical plane is as balanced as the horizontal, as in this instance,

SUSTAINABILITY

Sustainability can be about so much
more than processes, resources or
applications. It can be creative,
stimulating, challenging, funny,
underhand or extreme.

There are some phrases that mark an epoch, that reflect a moment in time and that pinpoint public mood, fashion or cultural woes. The term 'sustainable development' is one such phrase. Coined in the early 1980s by the Brundtland Commission, which looked into concerns about the human environment and its natural resources, it is a phrase that has been debated by academics and the public alike.

The term 'sustainable development' means meeting the needs of the present generation without compromising those of future ones. Although this may sound simple enough, the reality at a local, national or global level is significantly more challenging. Nearly 30 years after the Brundtland Commission report, the need to live by such a tenet has never been more urgent.

So what relationship does sustainable development have with a six-day flower show such as Chelsea? On the face of it, not a lot. After all, critics cry, this is a show that swallows significant amounts of money and resources in order to make what is in effect a temporary exhibition. And they would be right if it were not for one thing – the people creating the show gardens and nursery displays. Nearly everyone involved with the show, from the Royal Horticultural Society to a first-time exhibitor, from colleges in the Lifelong Learning displays to gardening product manufacturers, is aware of their demands on the planet and is increasingly conscious about doing something about it.

Those exhibiting in any capacity at Chelsea know that no other gardening show has comparable notoriety or media attention. As a result, many of the show garden themes centre around sustainability issues: from water harvesting to recycled products; and from drought-resistant planting to photovoltaic lighting. Sometimes entire gardens focus on a sustainable issue (see case study, p170). At other times, it might be small elements in

a show garden that suggest different ways of tackling things. Either way, the organisers require designers to explain how their gardens are sustainable.

Yet sustainability can be about so much more than processes, resources or applications. It can be creative, stimulating, challenging, funny, underhand or extreme. Designers and exhibitors revel in myriad possibilities, and rightly so. Sustainability needs to be imparted in a variety of ways and at different levels. For example, some gardeners may want to explore gardening organically, others may want to reduce their resource use (in terms of fertilisers or soil improvers). Some, who live in an urban environment have to plan and design their outside space minutely in order to get maximum sustainable use from it. Others, however, who may live in a larger rural garden, may not be so worried about space, but might find it easier to incorporate more composting facilities, fruit and vegetable growing, and diverse tree and plant selections. In other examples, some of the garden items (such as containers or paving) may be recycled or recyclable, while others may be considerably older but still in good condition. All these issues, and many more, meld into the pot of sustainability.

One of the many benefits of gardens is that together their sum is greater than the number of individuals. Also, studies such as the University of Sheffield's BUGS project (Biodiversity in Urban Gardens in Sheffield) have demonstrated the enormous repository

1 In its widest sense the word sustainability relates to how humans can live in harmony with their environment. Gardens play a crucial role in this, and small spaces especially so. Green roofs, mixed planting and space for wildlife are some of the key elements here.

2 Small things can really help make a difference. Here paving slabs have been interspersed with loose stones, allowing rainwater to drip through to the ground below. This is a great way to assist in keeping ground water levels topped up.

3 Water management is a very real issue in an outside space, especially for garden designers and city planners. Reducing excess run-off and dealing with the ebb and flow of water levels can be 'built' into a design with prior consideration.

that gardens can be for plants, wildlife and the environment in general. It is by designers reflecting on such findings, and then repackaging them for the benefit of the Chelsea audience, that such strong and important messages can be imparted.

For most gardeners, many of these issues are already everyday concerns. Therefore it is to the innovative ideas and new materials that gardeners should look when visiting Chelsea. Whether by planting green roofs (see p166) or using recycled car tyres as planters or raised beds; by introducing piles of logs to attract wildlife or including metal gabions filled with reclaimed industrial waste – designers will continue to explore the meaning of sustainability, and sustainable gardening. These are gardening realities that are set to be an increasingly important motif throughout many RHS Chelsea Flower Shows, and real life gardens, in the years to come.

4 Wildlife is crucial to biodiversity, and in turn to enhancing a garden's sustainability. Here a bee feeds off pollen in a *Cirsium rivulare* 'Atropurpureum' flower.

1

Sustainability as part of the plan

With climate change and environmental awareness now part of everyday life for most people, how you use your garden will become an increasingly important question. It means that what you grow, how you grow it, where you get your materials from and how you maintain them are very real issues. Such an approach, however, does not require you to grow large areas of nettles and make way for hordes of rabbits. Many clients of garden designers are demanding that their outside space be as sustainable as possible, whether it be by the ethical sourcing of natural stone or by introducing water storage and irrigation. Whatever the demands are, many designers are in a great position to help clients realise their environmental dreams. By balancing human needs with environmental concerns, both designers and gardeners can help develop a symbiotic relationship from a shared piece of land.

OVERALL IDEALS WITH NEW IDEAS

From intelligent manufacturing techniques through to overall design, gardens can respond well to sustainable demands.

1 The planting combinations, use of space and balance of materials in this garden make it a great example of sustainability, even though it didn't set out to be so labelled. After Chelsea, it was to be relocated to a hospice for children – in itself, a great act of recycling and reuse.

2 This scheme balances the needs of people with that of a thriving plant and animal community. Contemporary detailing is softened by the lush planting, as well as by pools of water (hidden from view) and structures for nesting birds and insects (integrated into the walls).

3 Front gardens can make an invaluable contribution to a street environment, by introducing a mixture of planting and materials to strong effect, as in this scheme, which cleverly combines personal space with wider society benefit.

4 Concrete manufacturing is known as being environmentally 'unfriendly'. To overcome this, the designers here used an innovative technique to reduce the carbon footprint of concrete manufacturing while creating their contemporary design.

Reusing materials

Possibly one of the most sustainable actions a gardener can do is recycle a product or material from their garden. For many gardeners this is nothing new – after all, home composting has been undertaken for years – yet Chelsea designers often offer new insights or suggestions for reusing materials. Whether old pots or sacks used to grow produce in, or broken containers stacked as wildlife homes, a range of actions can be taken that reduces the need for purchasing newly manufactured products. Clearly such a mantra can be challenging if you are after a modern contemporary scheme, but for most gardeners it is a highly realistic and achievable ambition. By considering what you have around you – and how you can use it – you are not only reducing your take on the environment but you are helping your wallet out too.

3

DESIGN FLAIR FROM EXISTING MATERIALS

A quick search in your garden or through local recycling centres can yield a range of great materials.

1 A combination of old roofing tiles, terracotta pots, timber pallets and bits of twig forms a great sanctuary for a range of wildlife, as well as being an interesting design feature. Such features can be temporary or long-term, depending on the level of construction skill, quality of materials and design need.

2 Stacked logs have been used for a boundary wall to a neighbouring property. The effect is compelling, but beware that, without sufficient thought before construction starts, such a structure is highly unstable. This particular wall was pinned for extra stability.

3 This 'living' tower, home to a wide range of wildlife, has been created by reusing bits of old wood, card and piping, as well as appropriate species of plants. As a result, it blends a sculptural design with a practical wildlife solution.

4 Old slate roofing tiles (reclaimed from a roof that was being renovated) have been set on edge to act as a highly textured pathway. The rusting steel-framed bench features timber made from old roof joists found in a reclamation yard.

4

EXPERT TIP
Nigel Dunnett Recycling water

❛ Water-related issues are going to become increasingly important to gardeners in the future, whether these are related to increased frequencies of intense summer drought or of torrential downpours and high flood risk. Water conservation is therefore very important. It can be undertaken in different ways: by altering planting types; by improving the moisture retention of your soil; or by leading to a change of planting ethos. A huge amount of water is lost from every house and garden as it runs away down the drains, both inside and outside the house. A water-efficient scheme aims to capture and utilise every drop of rainfall that falls on the house and garden, diverting water from roofs and downspouts into water butts and deflecting water run-off into planted areas and rain-fed ponds. Such an approach not only maximises the benefit to the garden, but it also reduces the contribution of all properties to overloading the drainage system in times of potential flood. Water recycling from the house – so-called grey water from washing dishes and using showers and baths – can be captured and used for irrigation, so long as 'eco-friendly' products have been used in the washing process. The ideal time to implement new water-saving devices or designs is when a project is being started, although it is possible to install products after a scheme has been finished. The outlay in costs may take some time to recoup, however. ❜

Copper pools add an ornamental touch to this garden, while at the same time having a useful role in retaining water collected from a nearby roof.

Attracting wildlife

Part of any successful ecosystem is the delicate balance of living organisms within a given area. For gardens to attract creatures – from the smallest insect to the largest garden mammal – they must provide food, shelter and the opportunity for that wildlife to make a home. You can easily help achieve this by introducing a range of habitats within your garden: from long grass to old pieces of decaying wood; from mixed planting to a pool of water. Turning your garden over to 'nature' while humans look on sounds for many people like ecospeak, yet that is far from the reality. What most gardeners, designers and Chelsea show gardens do is present a balance, where a range of materials are – by their very nature – different and are attractive to various parts of the wildlife spectrum. In so doing they are creating habitats that are well balanced, appealing to many creatures and continually sustainable as a result. By building and using a range of materials within a garden, a host of opportunities can be offered to wildlife, whether by supporting different types of plants (and as a result food sources) or for nesting in inanimate objects such as walls and eves.

LARGE AND SMALL, WILDLIFE FOR ALL

Whether planning a bee 'hotel' or an informal pond, wildlife encouragement should be an intrinsic part of any garden.

1 Clematis, rounded Allium heads and spires of white *Digitalis* are attractive, pollen-rich flowers for wildlife in late spring, and help give an informal, 'in tune with nature' feel to the space.

2 Keeping bees is an increasingly popular pastime, especially as bee populations across the world are in a state of decline. This garden shows how beautifully hives can be incorporated into a scheme.

3 These modern bird feeders have been set into a rendered wall – and should be squirrel-proof.

4 Another contemporary take, in the same garden as above, this time with solitary bee homes regularly spaced on a grey-blue wall.

5 A bound rope-house makes a small corner of this garden especially welcoming to wildlife.

6 Water is essential in any garden. This generous informal pond has shallow sides that allow wildlife easy access to the water, while the dense informal planting around it provides good cover for creatures.

Balancing aesthetics with nature's needs can be very challenging in a small garden. Good ideas include: native plants supporting a high level of biodiversity; pockets of water for visual impact and wildlife; and multistemmed trees, for shade.

Nature Ascending, Angus Thompson & Jane Brockbank, 2009

Statements with sustainability

Most people interested in creating sustainable gardens focus on the actions required rather than the message itself. Yet what defines a 'sustainable garden'? Because there is no one answer, garden owners and designers have demonstrated in various ways their understanding of the term. For some, a sustainable garden could be the one in which they use only organic materials to make their plants grow; for others it may be that all materials are sourced from within the existing garden space; and for yet more people it may be about increasing biodiversity. Chelsea gardens respond to all of these interpretations, and propose ideas – large and small – from using bountiful local materials as paving through to planting swathes of wild flowers.

RIBBONS OF COLOUR

Sustainable gardens should be as visually exciting as any other garden; they needn't be dull drab places.

1 This clever urban backdrop screen, with a wildflower seed mixture sown in front, shows how easy it is to beautify city spaces. Bringing plants to the urban environment not only helps reduce the dominance of hard surfaces, but it also entices wildlife in and can help reduce the overall urban heat island effect.

2 Use of locally adapted plants alongside soil conservation, composting and a natural approach to pest control are key messages in this garden, and are easily adopted by gardeners. Such plants need less man-made fertilisers or soil improvers to make them grow, as they have evolved over time in harmony with local conditions.

DETAILED ELEMENTS

Small touches evoking a specific memory, or perhaps imparting a meaningful message, can be rewarding to undertake in a home garden and are quite often easy to achieve.

1 Two takes on sustainability: home-grown vegetables reduce 'food miles', while old keys contribute to the path's make-up as well as help to impart this garden's theme of improving services for people who are homeless.

2 Old tyres have been planted with maroon-black-flowered *Zantedeschia*, while excess wheel nuts have been strewn as a mulch. (If doing this at home, ensure old tyres and nuts are clean and will not leak pollutants into the ground.)

3 An old car windscreen protects these tomato plants from rain damage, while the glass helps warm the area below and so maximises cropping.

GREENING ROOFS FOR GREAT EFFECT

Green roofs can be made at home, maybe on a garden shed or garage. Always check the structural integrity of the building before planting.

1 This green roof – planted primarily with *Sedum* species – brings a nice visual treat to the garden and is a great improvement on a building's usual roof tiles or tarred felt.

2 With some detailed planning and an awareness of what materials are most appropriate, a green roof can be 'retrofitted' to most garden buildings.

3 No space should be considered too small for making a contribution to greening up the environment. Here a wheelie bin storage cupboard has green vegetation on its roof.

Green roofs and living walls

One of the most significant additions to some of the Chelsea show gardens in recent years has been green roofs and living walls. Both concepts originate from the same premise: that, instead of looking at hard materials such as roof tiles or concrete, why not grow plants on that surface. Other advantages are also recognised: green roofs help keep buildings cool in summer and warm in winter; they have great aesthetic appeal; wildlife benefits from more plants growing in a given space; and green roofs especially can help with water (rainfall) absorption and (on a large scale) reduce local air temperature in summer. Chelsea designers have really adopted living walls and green roofs, and it is disappointing that planners and architects have not done so more in the public realm. Questions remain about the long-term nature of these plantings, but that shouldn't put people off.

WALLS THAT 'BREATHE AND GROW'

Appropriate plant selection and maintenance needs are particularly important considerations when planting up a wall.

1 This interesting scheme adapted the concept of a green wall by planting shrubs on top of the retaining structure as well. The result is a piece of great design.

2 Purple-leaved *Heuchera* is of significant colour value in this living wall, which runs diagonally from the planting bed upwards.

3 Leaf form, texture and understanding appropriate growth habits are essential ingredients for a successful green wall, as can be seen here by the use of *Alchemilla mollis*, *Armeria*, *Heuchera* and sage.

Diversity in planting

For most gardeners, it is the plants that soften the overall effect of a domestic garden, and bring visual interest and seasonal highlights. Plants also enhance the diversity of the garden, attracting a range of wildlife. In turn, this mix of wildlife sustains both predators and prey, again increasing the variety within the space. By including a range of plant types – from annuals to bulbs, shrubs to climbers, herbaceous perennials to trees –

microclimates can be achieved in the garden and these help the local environment while balancing the needs of other organisms sharing the soil space. Contemporary thinking has challenged the notion that 'native plants are best', instead suggesting that it is the range of plants in a given area that is of more use to wildlife. Whatever your view or planting preference, try to achieve a visual balance along with a sustained (year-round) approach.

EXPERT TIP
Nigel Dunnett Green roofs

❝ These are simply roofs that have had a layer of vegetation added to them. Garden sheds, porches, summerhouses, balconies, garages and small extensions all offer great potential for planting green roofs. Indeed, where garden or outdoor space is very restricted a green roof might be the only chance for bringing plants and wildlife into otherwise hard or built surroundings. The most important consideration for such a roof is how much weight the chosen building will support: it must comfortably take the weight of a person if it is to be strong enough to have a green roof planted on it; if you are in any doubt about this, do seek professional advice. The existing roof must also be waterproof. You can create a simple green roof by securing a pregrown mat of sedums over a pond liner on the roof surface, but it is preferable to plant individually into a generous layer of free-draining soil or potting compost on the roof. In addition to sedum species, many typical alpines such as *Dianthus* and thyme are excellent for green roofs, as are low-growing species tulips. Native wild flowers of chalk or limestone grassland, such as cowslip (*Primula veris*) and bird's foot trefoil (*Lotus corniculatus*), will increase the wildlife value of the roof. In partial shade, the range of plants can be increased to include alpine strawberries and ferns. Some watering may be necessary in very dry periods, and occasional weeding to remove unwanted plants. ❞

Plant in a minimum soil depth of 7.5cm (3in) on the roof.

Green roofs can be positioned in full sun or partial shade.

Before planting, spread a pond liner over a suitably strong, waterproof roof to protect it from plant root damage.

PLANTING IN DIFFERENT WAYS

In a sustainable scheme (as should be the case for all gardens), plant selection can be as important as the means by which the gardener will end up growing his or her selection.

1 A successful balance has been achieved here between 'soft' (plants) and 'hard' (paving) materials. The plants reduce the linearity of the paving, gravel and wall, while both the hard and soft elements help establish an attractive environment for wildlife.

2 A nice detail of thyme growing among paving slabs enhances this scene. Water can be absorbed through the herb while the paving provides convenient access across the garden.

3 Mixed planting is great for a balanced palette of vegetation. Growing ornamentals and productive plants together will become increasingly commonplace, especially as home gardens continue to decline in size.

4 If climate change predications become reality, gardens in cool-temperate areas may well be able to welcome some elements of this artificially created design – but not for some time yet.

THE MARSHALLS' SUSTAINABILITY GARDEN

Demonstrating 'sustainability' can be a real challenge. What is sustainable to one person may not be to the next. However, Chelsea designers have increasingly tried to show that considerate use of natural resources doesn't have to result in a garden that looks like an eco-junkyard. In this garden, the design team from Scenic Blue introduced a combination of materials and design ideas that were aimed at inspiring visitors. The result was a mixture of useful solutions for the home garden, backed up by a contemporary approach to outdoor space.

According to the designers, they wanted 'to appeal to consumers' consciences... who place increasing importance on issues relating to climate change, ethical and social values and the economic impact of globalisation'. These sound like worthy aims, but how do garden-related subjects manifest themselves as relating to climate change? Or social values?

ELEMENTS THAT MIGHT BE USED IN A DOMESTIC SETTING:

- the garden studio building incorporated into an earth-and-rubble bank not only utilises wasted space (and materials) but also uses the ground to help insulate/cool the building;
- solar panels have been set into futuristic-looking lighting housings, creating a bold visual statement of renewable energy;
- gabions can be filled with any material (depending on lateral weight), making interesting backdrops – they are also often useful homes for wildlife;
- a mixture of planting – from ornamental borders to longer, 'wild' grass atop the garden studio – benefits a range of wildlife and shows visual diversity in a small space;
- water is crucial for attracting wildlife as well as helping cool an outside space; in addition, the use of 'grey' (previously used) water to help feed the pond means no drains water need be called upon;
- hard landscaping, especially the Indian sandstone paving, has been sourced from independently verified ethical sources complying to the Ethical Trading Initiative Base Code (a strong message the garden's sponsor, Marshalls, wanted to get across).

The net result was a garden that demonstrated just what can be achieved at home. Whether it is lighting, water collection or reuse of materials, gardeners can make small steps to reduce their take on the environment, and this garden showed how easy it is.

5

DESIGNER Scenic Blue Design Team

CONTRACTOR Scenic Blue (UK)

AWARD Silver Flora

CATEGORY Show Garden, 2007

SPONSOR Marshalls plc

KEY WORDS recycled; sustainability; solar power; lifestyle; gabions; 'earth' building

IN A SENTENCE... A new take on a contemporary message, this garden aims to show that sustainability can fit into a modern design vernacular.

1 An informal and 'wild' grassland area on top of the earth mound forms one of two quite distinct sitting areas and contrasts markedly with the formal, hard landscaped deck in front of the building. Having spaces to sit in is often a primary and important motive for those making gardens.

2 By burying the garden building into an earth-and-rubble mound, the designers have managed to create a room out of unwanted material. The earth surrounding the building also helps insulate/cool the room below. The long grass and slight woodland feel on top contrast well with the modernity below.

3 Gabions are increasingly being used in garden making and rightly so: not only do they retain material, but their composition can also be of almost anything (depending on weight and component size). From old concrete slabs to roof slates, bits of wood to house bricks, their visual interest can match an existing space, and often become a benefit to a range of wildlife.

4 Solar power panels have been placed in contemporary and dramatic structures. These then harness the power for the sustainable LED lighting around the garden.

5 The crushed stone and Indian sandstone paving have been ethically sourced – a relatively new, and welcome, consideration for gardening consumers. Incorporating such materials to make a garden usable and accessible will become increasingly important for gardeners when creating outdoor spaces.

FUTURE NATURE

With more of the global population living in urban places, it is imperative that landscape architects, planners, architects, engineers and politicians grasp the urgent need to make cities as pleasurable to live in as possible. Infrastructure and planning are crucial, but so too are imaginative and practical solutions. By providing simple, useful and garden-friendly ideas here, Ark Design Management have shown that sustainability, environmental awareness and concern for urban developments can be visually stimulating... and environmentally beneficial.

Much of the current British work centred around greening urban environments – in terms of green roofs, public space seed mixtures and the use of sustainable resources – stems from work being undertaken in Sheffield, especially at the university of Sheffield. Research into understanding the urban environment, in tandem with the global scientific community's modelling information about climate change, is leading designers to understand better how gardens can help mitigate and adapt to fluctuations in weather. Just such a collaborative exercise was undertaken by the creators of this garden: horticulturist and ecologist Nigel Dunnett, architect Adrian Hallam and landscape architect Chris Arrowsmith. The result was an inspiring, enjoyable and successful garden.

CONSIDER THE IMPLICATIONS FOR DOMESTIC GARDENS:

- this garden aims to soak up, store and use every single drop of rainwater that falls onto the space – a key concern for anyone wanting to grow a range of plants in a limited outside space;
- planting and hard landscaping have been selected to deal with differing and sporadic levels of rainfall, so, for example, planting combinations are tough and some would need no irrigation in dry periods;
- wildlife, so vital to maintaining a healthy ecosystem, has plenty to feast upon, and endless opportunities in which to live (look at the central 'garden tower' to the left of the main picture);
- if buildings can be adapted to include a 'green' (planted) roof, then there are many possibilities. The benefit is not only visual – who would rather see roof tiles than a mixture of planting? – but also practical in terms of water storage, pollution absorption and planting diversity;
- the inclusion of water pools and rills – whether permanent or seasonal – creates visual interest and can also substantially boost wildlife.

This garden demonstrated many small-scale yet big-impact steps individuals can take to help counter the ongoing changes to our climate. Wouldn't it be a better place if all urban areas started to look a little like this?

1 Drainpipes are used to direct any excess roof water onto the planting below. Green roofs help absorb and slow down the rate of storm water that would otherwise fall directly onto roads and buildings, and end up in the sewer system.

2 This 'living' tower provides plants and animals with space and a refuge. By incorporating a range of materials, sizes and textures, the attraction for fauna is maximised. In a home garden, a variety of unwanted materials could be used to dramatic effect.

DESIGNERS Ark Design Management (Adrian Hallam, Chris Arrowsmith and Nigel Dunnett)

CONTRACTOR Dendale, Galemain Engineering, M&SE

AWARD Silver-Gilt Flora

CATEGORY Show Garden, 2009

SPONSOR Yorkshire Water, University of Sheffield Alumni Fund, Green City Initiative and Buro Happold

KEY WORDS sustainability; urban; roof garden; eco-awareness; water management; biodiversity

IN A SENTENCE... A great suite of water-based ideas for planting and designing in an urban environment.

3 A photograph of a city scene has been used as the backdrop to this garden, to help give a sense of scale and reality to the design. Considering the views beyond your garden, or the context in which your creation sits, is essential, whether it be to maintain pleasant views or to introduce plantings to block out eyesores.

4 A series of pools and rills occurs beyond this planting, demonstrating how water can be incorporated into the smallest of spaces, as well as the invaluable role plants have in water purification, stormwater retention and for wildlife.

5 White-stemmed birches (*Betula utilis*) give height and a sense of maturity at the back of the garden. These trees represent the diversity of plants often seen in urban brownfield sites. At home, garden trees are vital for interest and scale, but choose carefully as some are better suited to smaller spaces than others.

6 The planting is a stylised meadow, with native and non-native plants, several of which colonise urban wasteland, yet it has a beautiful and 'planterly' effect. In your garden, consideration of soil, aspect, wildlife attraction and irrigation must be given to ensure that the maxim of 'right plant, right place' is adhered to at all times.

PRODUCTIVE GARDENS

Growing your own can be
one of the most satisfying
and rewarding parts of
any gardener's craft.

One of the most significant revivals that has taken place in recent years has been the renewed interest in 'growing your own' (GYO). As a reaction to the post-Second World War years of hardship and frugalness, and the excitement and technological innovation of the 1970s and 80s, home-grown fruit and vegetables had become something of a distant memory – until the past decade.

And what a revival it has been. Suddenly everybody is interested in growing some element of food, whether fruit, herbs or vegetables in a container, raised bed or in the ground. Allotment waiting lists run into years in some parts of the country, while schools and communities are being encouraged to come together to make space for food growing. Books, websites and magazines have focused on the topic for everyone from novice to the experienced. But where and how does the RHS Chelsea Flower Show fit into this – has it been able to keep up with this burgeoning interest? Indeed it has, by demonstrating very well the aesthetic and benefits of including fruit and veg. The main challenge for nurserymen and designers when wanting to include crops in their gardens is the timing of the show. As a result many of the plants at Chelsea are forced. By the third week of May, when the show

takes place, fruit and vegetables are normally only in very early growth. Even with the most advanced growing conditions for making plants think it is actually July instead of May, it is still a considerable feat to be able to grow crops that are of a sufficient size, quality and number for show purposes. As ever with Chelsea show gardens, some years this growing trick can work brilliantly; in other years weather and bad luck may just be against the grower.

The end result is that productive gardening at Chelsea is demonstrated in many ways, and all of them usually applicable to a domestic situation. In some, the growing area occupies the whole garden, suggesting that a conventional space doesn't have to be confined to ornamental plants – it can be about seasonal vegetables, summer berries, culinary herbs or wildlife-haven fruit trees. At other times, designers include raised beds or containers that suggest smaller scale changes. But no matter the size or scale of the growing area, gardeners must always consider what they want to grow, how much they will want of it, and what soil type and aspect each crop will need. Once they have considered these essentials, the possibilities for including vegetables or fruit into the garden are endless.

One of the really exciting developments in productive growing over the past 30 years or so has been the expansion of seed and plant availability. Whereas in the middle of the 20th century people would have considered Brussels sprouts, cabbages and runner beans staple

1 Productive gardening can bring colour, shape and texture to a garden, as well as delicious, home-grown food.

2 Chelsea designers often incorporate fruit and vegetables to great effect in their show gardens, and in so doing recreate utopian images of how many of us might like our veg patch to be.

3

3 **Growing fruit**, vegetables and herbs is a hugely rewarding undertaking, often with gardeners nurturing plants from a few packets of seeds to full-blown, harvestable crops.

garden produce in the UK, gardeners are now treated to an international menu – from Thai or Asian vegetables to Mediterranean citrus; South American sweet potatoes to Italian salad leaves; bean sprouts to micro-, baby- or teen-leaf lettuce; and increasingly popular 'superfruits' (such as blueberries) to fruit trees grown on dwarfing rootstock, which are ideal for smaller gardens.

How they are used is also being explored. From mixing crops with ornamentals to growing serried ranks of unusual herbs, from planting strawberries in colanders (see p184) to growing vegetables on vertical surfaces (see p182), designers' imagination will continue to challenge perception and inspire supporters.

Increasingly, growing things – whether productive or ornamental – is being appreciated as an enjoyable pastime. Fruit or veg is a great way of encouraging children to get their hands dirty and give it a go.

Ingenious and simple little touches come from the creative fingers of Chelsea designers, for children (see p184). Community-based projects, national media coverage and education-based guidance, such as the RHS Campaign for School Gardening, strive to reconnect children, and those from disadvantaged backgrounds, with the food they eat.

Ultimately, this is inspiration that Chelsea must provide. With continued interest in reducing 'food miles', the constant uncertainty on international food pricing and stability, and a greater awareness of the husbandry of food, gardeners will need shows like Chelsea to push boundaries and try new ideas. Coupled with the sheer beauty and interest in productive crops, this show will undoubtably demonstrate over the coming years that growing your own can be one of the most satisfying and rewarding parts of any gardener's craft.

Growing your own

The aesthetic appeal they can bring to a garden is often one of the forgotten benefits of growing fruit and veg. All that energy, colour, shape, texture and different growth habits can be found in one small area, bringing together produce that originated from different parts of the world into your back garden. The other self-evident benefit is that with a bit of foresight, due care and attention and some luck, most gardeners can establish and raise crops successfully to produce home-grown fare. Taste, freshness, quality, reduced 'food miles' and a huge amount of satisfaction combine to make growing your own a great way to spend some or all of your gardening time.

EXPERT TIP
Jekka McVicar
How to grow herbs

'As a general rule, Mediterranean herbs such as thyme (*Thymus vulgaris*), sage (*Salvia officinalis*), oregano (*Origanum vulgare*), savory (*Satureja montana*) and French tarragon (*Artemisia dracunculus* French) like to be planted in full sun in a well-drained soil. The reason full sun is required is that it is the sun that brings the herbs' essential oils to the surface of the leaf, and it is these oils that make the herbs taste so good in the kitchen. An important tip for keeping these herbs productive for regular use in the kitchen is to cut the plants back after flowering. This will encourage new growth and, with the exception of the tarragon as it is herbaceous, will give you leaves for use in the winter months. Increasingly, gardeners are intermingling herbs with their ornamental plantings, and there are many different selections of herbs to link them in visually.'

This 'herb wheel' is a great addition to any garden, bringing together thyme, salvia, oregano and parsley for use in the kitchen.

STYLE TO SUIT ALL TASTES

Productive gardens, large or small, can balance both visual style and personal growing preference.

1 Blue-painted planters of different heights visually co-ordinate a range of crops, from leeks to courgettes, beetroot to apple trees.

2 This formal, classic scheme unusually uses low, woven-willow-edged raised beds in conjunction with high-quality paving, and a beautiful greenhouse (for establishing young plants) in the distance.

3 A herb bed on top of an outside storage cupboard is a simple idea that is not only useful but also clean and contemporary in style.

Raised beds

Originally introduced into areas of poor or heavy soil, raised beds were built above ground level and filled with new, better soil, so as to allow crops to grow well. However, over time this practical response to poor soil has almost become the norm, with more and more gardeners opting for raised beds to contain their productive gardening. Not only is soil quality much easier to manage in a raised bed, but so too are maintenance issues of keeping edges neat and by weeding being more convenient because the beds are higher off the ground. In true Chelsea fashion, designers continue to push the creative boundaries of what materials constitute a raised bed, and what can be grown within them.

1

2

FROM THE GROUND UPWARDS

Consider the amount of growing space you need for your crops, and then devise raised beds to meet that requirement.

1 These herbs (rosemary, thyme, sage and lemon balm) are well set off by a curved blue metal planter.

2 Chives and bronze fennel, in the nearest woven-willow-edged raised bed, with cardoons in the second bed, combine for a visual feast.

3 A raised, plinth-like planter doubles up as a bench and somewhere to fill with productive vegetation – in this instance a 30-year-old, late-flowering apple tree growing from within it.

4 A contemporary take on veg growing in a small space – a steel tray, filled with mature cos lettuce.

5 Strong colour and foliage textures abound in this small space held together by a white painted wall.

Gardening for a beautiful bounty

The joy of growing your own can bring different ages, cultures and abilities together. Just as with ornamental planting, productive gardening can represent your personal interests; it can reflect the style of your overall garden, respond to needs and tastes, and can help you understand the relationship between garden and soil. In all, productive gardening can be a hugely rewarding experience, where successes are greeted with glee and delight, and failures met with a steely determination to try something different next time. Growing your own is not always easy, and problems are often encountered, but when a seed germinates or your first tomato is ready to pick, it brings a smile to even the most experienced of growers.

4

GETTING THE MOST FROM YOUR SPACE

Maximising use of space is crucial if a garden is to yield a crop of fresh and healthy plants.

1 This novel kitchen garden concept explores the possibility of growing fruit and veg in a small space, on walls and surfaces, really hitting home the link between 'kitchen' and 'garden'.

2 Many vegetables, here such as lettuce, can be grown closely together for immediate and ongoing harvesting.

3 With well-used space and a lot of hard work, a produce-laden garden can be achieved, ensuring garden owners have a fresh supply of food for many months of the year.

4 Lettuce, beans and tomatoes jostle together in a small corner of this garden and are enhanced by a sunny sunflower.

Contained excitement

Increasingly, those gardeners with small outside spaces are being offered the opportunity to share in the 'grow-your-own revolution'. Whether it be by choosing specially bred cultivars that grow smaller, or via growing systems that use soil and water to maximum effect, the owner of a small garden can really get stuck into growing produce. And the beauty of veg, especially, is that it doesn't care what it is being grown in – a row of lettuces in an old plastic container will be just as happy as they would be in the ground, as long as feeding, watering and husbandry are kept to the normal standard. Growing produce in containers is also a great way of involving children, allowing them to garden at their physical height, as well as in defined areas that are not too onerous. Whatever your passion, or your palette, growing your own in a container is a viable, enjoyable way of running a kitchen garden.

CONTAINERS CAN BRING A WEALTH OF GROWING OPPORTUNITY

No matter what the container is and where it is placed – on a windowsill or in a courtyard – it can be used to grow fresh produce in any garden.

1 Crops can be grown in a range of containers, some small enough for just one plant.

2 Cress in old egg shells is just one novel idea to get children involved with growing and is a great way of introducing them to gardening.

3 This fun idea marries fruit (strawberries) with a kitchen implement (colander). By hanging the colander planter above a table, it is easy to pick the delicious fruit from underneath.

4 Pot-grown citrus plants can be brought outdoors during the summer months to help fruit ripen, as they do best in a sunny warm position.

EXPERT TIP

Jekka McVicar
Planting up a container for summer salad crops

'Salad rocket (*Eruca vesicaria* subsp. *sativa*), dill (*Anethum graveolens*) and mustard (*Brassica juncea*) are all great salad herbs that can be easily raised from seed and grown in a container. The trick is to choose a planter large enough to grow a crop for cutting; an ideal size is 23cm (9in) wide by 18cm (7in) high, or 5 litres/1 gallon, or larger. Fill with compost and water well, then sow the seeds and cover lightly with more compost. Set the container in a sheltered warm spot that is shaded from the midday sun. Once you start cutting your salad, feed the plants every week with a balanced liquid fertiliser. This will help them to develop productive succulent growth.'

Growing vegetables in raised planters gives physically easy access while allowing soil to be free-draining and easily improved.

SUMMER SOLSTICE

Getting a message across is often a key requirement for a sponsor, but it can sometimes get 'lost in translation' in the actual garden. Not so here. This immaculately executed display reflected the sponsor's vision for high-quality materials, organic principles and clean design. For some, this was not a garden but an idealised version of an agrarian landscape comfortably existing side by side with a potager and outdoor kitchen. But, at Chelsea, such an approach can make a garden, and this fine example showed how big design statements – a 'field' of green wheat, raised vegetable beds and a green-roofed building – not only give inspiration but also reflect a deeper ethos.

This was the first time that the design partnership of del Buono Gazerwitz had entered Chelsea. Their design style of clean lines and simple spatial combinations translated well into this space. The balance of areas, combinations of materials and strong ethos underlying the show garden's creation reinforced a message that any gardener at home can undertake. At the core, though, was the need to be consistent and dogged; the designers and sponsor here wanted to remind gardeners of the 'vital importance of nurturing the soil and preserving it for future generations', and they have made sure every detail rings true to that.

MUCH CAN BE LEARNED FROM THIS SCHEME:

- even in a relatively small space (210 square metres/250 square yards), you can have two distinct areas: the wheat 'field' (see inset) and a vegetable garden;
- by including two quite different spaces, the plot can feel a lot bigger than its crude dimensions suggest;
- the use of quality materials – such as the raised vegetable beds or green roof on the outdoor building – reinforce a message of longevity and craftsmanship;
- a 'rural' style can easily be created in a contemporary and modern way;
- having, in close proximity, a cooking area, fresh produce and a building happily facilitates 'outdoor living';
- green roofs can be applied to many buildings, providing visual interest as well as environmental benefits;
- fruit and vegetables can take a lot of work (especially to look this good) so be prepared for some failures, some successes and a lot of hard work.

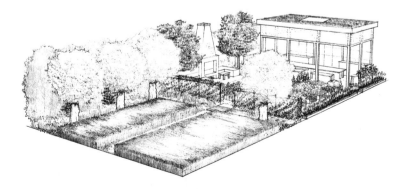

1 Rustic-style, woven plant supports materially link with the raised beds, allowing tomatoes to grow up through them. Such vertical accents are needed to give scale and drama to this beautiful sea of vegetable and fruit growing. As most vegetables are grown in just one year, the following year something completely different could grow up the supports: maybe some runner beans, climbing gourds or ornamental sweet peas.

DESIGNER Tommaso del Buono and Paul Gazerwitz; Spencer Fung Architects

CONTRACTOR Brambles Garden Landscapes

AWARD Silver-Gilt Flora

CATEGORY Show Garden, 2008

SPONSOR Daylesford Organic

KEY WORDS country; rural; quality details; contemporary feel; outdoor kitchen; craft

IN A SENTENCE... A two-part garden, linking the wider landscape with productive horticulture, underpinned by quality construction.

2 The healthy, diverse and interesting range of crops – from chives to cardoons, parsley to cabbages – contributes to the success of this space, as does the simplistic but beautifully executed design. Many people would deem this their idealised vision of a vegetable garden.

3 This outdoor fireplace could be used for cooking freshly harvested produce or more ornamentally as an outdoor fire, ready to be relaxed next to after eating a plentiful meal. Either way, it adds a grand focal point to the wall and the whole growing area, and it reinforces the link between organic crop growing and culinary uses.

4 A rough, hoggin-like path divides the raised growing beds, bringing a sense of gridded formality to all the energy being displayed by the crops. Paths and access are crucial for veg plots: make sure the paths between beds are big enough to allow for a smooth passage. In many instances this may need to be wide enough for a wheelbarrow.

5 A simple grass path in the front end of the garden leads up to a hand-made gate (decorated with a rustic heart shape) and on into the productive garden. Although still underpinned by organic principles, in the front garden the designers show us the agrarian landscape, a field of green wheat gently swaying in the wind.

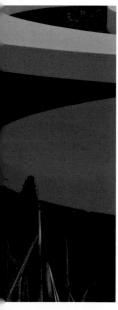

LIGHTING

Chelsea gardens show that whole new effects can be created outside by well-planned, and responsibly used, light.

The concept of the 'room outside' has been around since the 1960s, when leading garden designer John Brookes established it as a term that gardeners could understand. In a sense, the term 'room outside' gave people permission to consider their gardens as spaces that could be embellished, beautified or used for relaxation. As a result they became places for creative expression.

Nowhere is this decorative trend more true than with the development of garden lighting. By its very nature, using lights in a garden extends the amount of time that can be spent outdoors – it allows owners to use their outside space at the flick of a switch. Sitting in your garden, surrounded by some well-positioned lights, enjoying the evening ambience, can create a whole new relationship with your environment. At night – or early in the morning – the mass and voids, structure and form, colour and texture can become 'invisible' because they are not illuminated; and the end result is something quite different.

So what sort of lighting should be considered for a garden, and how have Chelsea designers included it? In recent years innovation has allowed them to really experiment with lighting; long gone are the days of large coloured bulbs pointing directly at a tree. As well as mains-fed lights, photovoltaic lighting (powered by the sun) has improved greatly in recent years, and substantially in design – originally their light was a musky yellow, but now a much clearer white light is given out.

Nowadays, gardens can have 'washes' of light to highlight the important, add drama to the ordinary and illuminate the necessary. Chelsea show gardens use just such principles to great effect (see case study, p200) – on a dramatic sculpture here or a water feature there. And in a way, it is this understanding of how lighting can enhance and improve a space that has 'powered' the substantial technical advancement in garden lighting. Chelsea gardens show us, as does the lighting industry, that whole new effects can be created outside by intelligent use of light.

A number of considerations are crucial before lighting your garden: you must think about which areas you want or require illuminated, and how that might be achieved; garden illumination isn't about having as many lights outside as possible. In addition, consideration should be given to neighbours or adjacent spaces. So too should there be concern for wildlife and energy use, especially if the lights are to be kept on at night. You should mix into the blend the need to plan and design for trunking and wiring, as well as the necessity that garden lighting must be fitted by a qualified professional electrician.

But what gardeners gain from Chelsea is, as is so often the case, a bag full of ideas. Over the years, the inclusion of lighting in show gardens has increased, to the point now where it is possible that most displays will include some lights. Undertaken well, and with attention to detail, lighting gardens can be an art form in itself. A little time working out what you want to illuminate, and by how much, will substantially increase your enjoyment when you sit down – one night – in your garden surrounded by washes of beautiful light.

1 **Accentuating the vertical** form in a garden is a common use of garden lighting. Here, a light placed at the base of a silver birch not only illuminates the branches and structure of the tree but also highlights the clean white trunk.

2 Coloured lighting can be used to strong effect in gardens, though consider its use carefully – the 'wrong' type or application of a colour can look tacky. Here the folds in the sculpture help reduce the block of colour, adding texture and shadows to the overall impression.

3 The lighting techniques in this classical view can be applied to a range of garden settings: the urn in the foreground uplit, with the same technique mirrored on the sculpture behind. They focus attention on exactly what you – the creator – wants visitors to see.

ALL PART OF THE PLAN

Whether lighting a building or a tree, consider how and what role you need garden lights to play.

1 This clever scheme continues the atmospheric lighting from the outside space to the indoor garden room.

2 An ambient feel to this seating area has been created by backlighting the planting behind while focusing other lights onto the 'sails' above.

3 With a detailed approach to illumination, such as here, you can single out important parts of the night-time garden.

Illuminating effects

Lights can be used in two principal ways in a garden: as a means of illuminating a specific object (see p194) or as a facility for shedding light across a larger area. For the latter, it is necessary to work out exactly what you want to be illuminated, how that effect may take place and what any by-products of that lighting may be. For the former, identify how you want the object lit and consider how that element may change appearance when artificially illuminated.

It is now well understood that when a large single light is placed in a garden its illumination is both unsympathetic and visually unappealing within the area. Therefore, it is far better to understand how light works and what mood and ambience you want your garden to have at night-time. If possible, use freestanding lights while determining your scheme; then when you are ready to install them permanently, you can be sure that your desires will come true.

EXPERT TIP
Tony Craddock Light sources

' The four main types of primary light sources commonly used for gardens are as follows:

- LED (light emitting diode) offers a wide choice of colours: white, blue, red, green, amber and colour-change versions. The bulbs have a long life, are cool to touch and have low running costs.
- High-pressure sodium is complementary to reds and yellows (such as red-leaf copper beech and *Prunus* trees). Sandstone and traditional brickwork also benefit from sodium lighting.
- Halogen creates a warm atmosphere and is associated with the natural environment. Despite its shorter life, it is the best choice for illuminating domestic plants and foliage.
- Metal halide is probably the best 'all rounder' light source, with its relatively long bulb life as well as its light spectrum resembling natural daylight, which makes it an especially good choice for revealing objects in their true colours. '

[above] LED lights illuminate a flight of steps, providing gentle guidance rather than blinding people as they pass through the space.

[left] This halogen spotlight uplighter is a discreet but effective way of focusing onto a tree or sculpture.

3

Lighting the specific

The main challenge when lighting a garden is understanding exactly what will and will not be illuminated. In the daytime this is difficult to predict, so trial and error are necessary when finalising your lighting scheme. To get the best from your garden, a range of styles and applications can be used, from specific small-scale spotlighting to swashes of colour against a wall or flight of steps. Many lighting appliances can be bought from local shops or the internet, but make sure that they are fitted by trained electricians who understand the appliances.

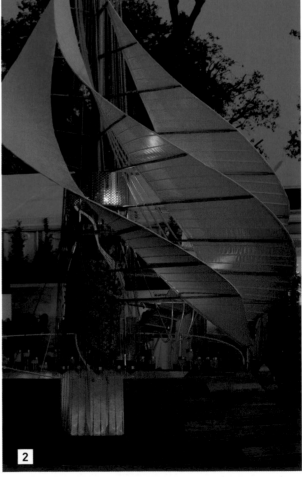

DEFINITION IN WORK

Colour can be achieved in different ways, either by the bulb light itself or by the illumination of a coloured object.

1 Simple, ground-level highlights, here in blue-mauve, make the natural white of the birch bark have an almost ghostly appearance.

2 This unusual and substantial sculpture is enhanced by night-time illumination; note how the colours change as it falls on different parts of the creation, using shadows and intensity to great effect.

INTO SHARP RELIEF

Whether it is a spotlight on a tree or a path light illuminating steps, a range of products can be used to enhance the garden.

1 As night falls, artificial lights begin to illuminate a vegetable planter and associated wall. Their low level, on the ground plan and within the planting, gives a soft and relaxed atmosphere, and makes the whole space feel particularly accessible during evening.

2 This Japanese-inspired lantern provides a diffused light in a dark corner. Note how much more subtle the lighting effect is here, when compared with more self-conscious spotlights. Always try to hide or at least reduce from view an appliance's bulb – its glare can ruin a night-time illumination.

3 Glass tiles lit from underneath the floor of a patio reveal their interesting and considered detail. The gentle light created helps people move over the space easily.

EXPERT TIP

Tony Craddock
Employing an electrician

Consulting a qualified electrician is the best way to ensure that you get exactly the garden lighting scheme you want.

' Garden lighting can be complicated and should be done by qualified professionals. Indeed, in many countries it is now illegal for anyone other than a qualified electrician to install and maintain a lighting scheme (in the UK, this is known as 'Part P' of Building Regulations). Such electricians can be sourced through professional trade associations. Be clear with them about what you want, and always check on how long the job is likely to take. Before giving the go-ahead for the lighting scheme, you should consider the implications that armoured trunking will need to be laid deeply enough so as not to be caught when digging over a bed. For a short time, this may mean moving plants. You will also need easy access to circuits and primary switches located indoors. '

Aqua dramatics

In everyday life, water and electricity do not normally mix. But thanks to great advancements in technological engineering – plus some clever visual trickery – water can be illuminated to create amazing garden scenes. The effect can be startling, bold, refined or enchanting. The most common appliances are submerged lights, placed below the water level, whereby depth and a bright white light can be introduced. Other lighting techniques involve the careful placement of appliances under or within fountains or jets; in more pared-down schemes, lights can be used to give a discreet wash of colour near or on the water's surface. Fitting such lighting requires a competent professional electrician who understands the demands of the lighting, and water feature, throughout the gardening year. Ensure maintenance is easy to carry out on fuse boxes, switches and appliances.

[right] Uplighters can be set within a lawn so that they shine directly up and underneath a tree canopy – the effect is eye-catching, contemporary and pleasantly welcoming.

[far right] Night-time lighting can be used to highlight details (here, a tree trunk) that during the daylight hours might be overlooked.

EXPERT TIP
Tony Craddock
Lighting techniques

❝ A wide range of light fixtures and styles can give an array of night-time views. Consider what you want the effect to be, and how the light sources may practically be subsumed into the garden. Lighting can be used to make different impacts:

- Downlighting replicates the way light (sunlight) is perceived, and it is especially effective when used in structures such as pergolas or from canopies.

3

4

LIGHTING THAT EBBS AND FLOWS

Whatever the effect required, garden lighting is one way in which you can make a water feature come alive.

1 The drama of the arched water feature is exacerbated by the illumination of the circular pool below, while the back lighting against the canopy in the corner encourages night-time use.

2 Strips of blue lights against the pool edge create a contemporary and unusual display. Water plays a subtle role here, gently flowing around the raised planters.

3 Diamond-sawn paving slabs appear to float above the water, their form and texture accentuated by the subtlety of light – the sources of which are hidden in this view.

4 Full-on shock and awe are created in this two-tier water feature. The top pool and jets seem to be burning bright white, while the vertical waterfall glows blue. The net result is a great water feature that can be appreciated throughout the whole evening.

- Uplighting – when a lighting fixture is placed under an object such as a tree or sculpture – creates an overall wash of illuminated space. Recessed uplight fixtures are very discreet.
- Spotlighting is a direct lighting technique used to illuminate important features such as statuary.
- Path lighting is generally subtle and is for illuminating the horizontal plane; it gives direction and helps people avoid tripping on potential hazards such as steps.
- Silhouetting, as seen in nature at sunset, is when an object is between the viewer and setting sun; use wide-beam light sources placed behind planting or objects to create this effect. ❯

The role of lighting in bringing this garden into night-time use has been executed with style and drama. Cold blue accentuates the planting at ground level and lights the sculptural daisies, while clear 'white' lights make the garden building fully usable.

The Oceânico Garden, Diarmuid Gavin and Sir Terence Conran, 2008

THE OCEÂNICO GARDEN

Some designers are notorious before they even get to the RHS Chelsea Flower Show, and Irish designer and television presenter Diarmuid Gavin was one such, as was designer, restaurateur and writer Sir Terence Conran. In this combined creation, they have successfully shown how the feel and look of a garden can be changed between day and night-time. To make the place feel truly enjoyable, they defined the effects they wished to create, colours they could use and lighting appliances they needed. By early planning, gardeners too can make sure their hard and soft landscaping looks just as good in the day as at night.

The intention for this design was to create a city courtyard 'that invites visitors to stop for a cup of coffee, a glass of wine or a light lunch'. At its heart, a metal and timber pavilion (complete with base-hinged sides to protect the building from bad weather) overlooks a densely planted 'sea' of planting – box balls abound, softened and supported by purple-flowered alliums and feathery *Stipa tenuissima*. To make the maximum use of this space, lighting has been introduced throughout to highlight further the principal design features. The result is a garden, during the day, that is full of whites, greens and the odd dash of purple; but by night a consistency of colour swallows the planting and walls, with lighting bringing relief to the dark green and black.

SOME KEY LESSONS FOR GARDENERS:

- think of how you want to use your garden during a 24-hour period, and if lighting is needed understand what you need illuminated, and how;
- successful lighting, as seen here, is more often about the effect created rather than the appliances creating it – many designers like to hide the lighting fixture so the illumination is achieved in a more subtle manner;
- colour lighting, once the garish pursuit of 1970s and 1980s designers, does have its place, but beware of overusing it and ensure that the colours introduced complement (or properly contrast with) not only each other but also their subjects;
- if you have bold sculptural statements in your garden (such as the metal mesh 'daisies' here), consider how they can 'come alive' at night and what type of lighting will make the most of their form;
- safety issues of lighting (both installation, which should be carried out by a qualified electrician, and ongoing maintenance) must be considered from the outset. Also think how electrical cables can be incorporated into the scheme.

1 White metal mesh daisy 'flowers' bring shade and a sense of seclusion/safety at ground level during the day, while at night-time the designers have accentuated their form by focusing the beam of light onto their undersides (see previous page), accentuating their physical shape and channelling the visitor's view to the pavilion.

DESIGNER Diarmuid Gavin and
Sir Terence Conran

CONTRACTOR Richard Hill, Basewood
Designs

AWARD Bronze Flora

CATEGORY Show Garden, 2008

SPONSOR The Oceânico Group

KEY WORDS box mounds; sculptural
'daisies'; lighting; outdoor café; texture

IN A SENTENCE... An outside space that
mixes a simple planting palette with fun
shade structure 'daisies' and interesting
night-time lighting.

2 The outdoor pavilion can seem somewhat shaded, with natural low light levels filtering in. However, at night, the building is much brighter, lit to make it perfectly usable for entertaining, relaxing or working in. Note the contrast between the bright light of the internal walls of the building (acting as a visual focus) and the surrounding, more subdued light in the garden.

3 Small spots of light directed at ground level accentuate not only the mounds of the box balls but also the purple allium flowerheads. These lights are in addittion to the back lighting or highlighting that has been carried out in this garden.

4 A dense backdrop of *Prunus laurocerasus* foliage brings a darkness to the garden. However, come evening, lighting effects accentuate both foliage and trunk, giving a more mystical and visually interesting backdrop to the pavilion. Note also that by using the same colour to illuminate the front and back of the garden, consistency is achieved.

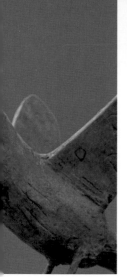

ART IN
THE GARDEN

In essence, this is an artistic display or creation that uses materials to symbolise, highlight or adorn your garden.

For thousands of years, mankind has personalised and adorned his immediate surroundings. From long-standing symbolic religious embellishments to seasonal displays, people have used both the precious and the commonplace to give identity to a space. Whether it be for a day or for a lifetime, gardeners and artists alike have used a vast array of materials for serious and humorous purposes.

In a modern context, such a basic human desire to decorate, augment or personalise a garden has never been more apparent. From mass-market, garden-centre products to bespoke pieces of one-off artwork, consumers are increasingly buying artefacts that can be sited outside. The RHS Chelsea Flower Show demonstrates this only too well; there, the gardens generally include artwork to support or define a design, and there are also many sundry stands displaying sculpture, water features or furniture.

So, what can be considered 'art in the garden'? In essence, it is an artistic display or creation that uses materials to symbolise, highlight or adorn your garden. As with paintings, artistic appreciation is highly personal, so for some people a collection of old-fashioned terracotta pots lined up on a windowsill would define 'art'; for others, it may be the inclusion of expensive, one-off sculptures displayed to maximum effect. In another garden, stone figures that you chance upon may be more subtle than a row of flags fluttering boldly in the wind, yet the enjoyment and appreciation they give may be the same – but for different people. It is this breadth of consumers that Chelsea manages to relate to.

It is unsurprising that many sections of society are wanting to purchase and enjoy such a range of art, especially now that they are becoming more media savvy, with the ever-swirling mass of information the internet provides. Television and papers too are exploring design in much greater detail.

Show gardens tend to include artworks either as adornment and addition, or as an integral part of the overall design. For the former, it is perhaps easier to see how lessons can be learned for the gardener. In such gardens, designers may include a water feature that ebbs and flows on a constant rhythm; a sculpture that relates to surrounding flower colour or hard landscaping; or a piece of wall-mounted *trompe-l'oeil* that acts as a focal point. These are one-off elements, bought, placed and viewed primarily as single pieces.

More challenging, both spatially and financially, is the inclusion of artworks to help define an entire space. Consideration must be given as to what you want the artwork to achieve in the space; what it might look like; how you will relate to it over time (and how it will weather); as well as practical concerns such as security and fixings.

The role producers and manufacturers play in inspiring the gardening public should not be underestimated. Not only do they display what can be bought, but in so doing they suggest ideas that people might otherwise have not been aware of. Mirrors, for example, can be placed in a garden to extend the feeling of space, as long as they are located in a suitable place and reflect features worthy of highlighting; sculptures, likewise, can be placed anywhere in a garden, giving a bold- or low-key statement. Paint effects (either as wall colour or subtle highlights) can bring a new dimension to a space, as can recycling materials to create visual interest.

1

1 Artworks come in all shapes and materials, and can be large-scale or small. Here an array of colours and textures – gravel, plants, and rough-hewn and smoothed wood – combine to bold and eye-catching effect.

2 Discreet pieces of art are becoming increasingly common in gardens, but how they are positioned, and what next too, are important concerns. Here the bowing man looks as if he is ready to smell the white-flowered lily next to him.

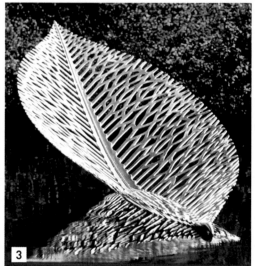

A sense of 'stage set' is also evident at the RHS Chelsea Flower Show – the odd unplanted terracotta urn here, or a collection of twigs there – to give an impromptu but artful contribution. The net result is an air of creativity at Chelsea that stimulates the senses and gets gardeners thinking about their next purchase or their own home-made artwork.

In financial terms, garden artworks can range from those that are totally free to those costing thousands of pounds. There are now myriad artisans, creators and designers willing to work with clients to produce whatever is required, whether it be made from wood, steel, bronze, glass, Perspex or other materials. However, art in the garden should be about more than flash statements or 'cheque-book gardening': it should reflect the spirit of the owners, relate to their likes and dislikes, and be just as important as hanging a picture above a fireplace indoors. What matters is that you enjoy the artwork for what it is. Whether a painted wall or bronze, life-size horse's head, a highly decorated dividing screen or a slowly decaying stone sculpture... artworks in the garden should be as individual as the individuals owning them. And for those people, Chelsea never disappoints.

3 When combined, materials – here, metal and water – can substantially increase the sum of a sculpture's parts. This sculptural leaf seems to float gently on the smooth water surface, belying the actual complexities of ensuring that this balancing act is executed to perfection.

4 Large sculptures such as this are dominant focal points in a garden, and need to be sited with care and attention. Note how the screen behind softens the overall effect, blurring the depth and edging of the glass mass, thereby reducing its overall impact.

Location, location

How and where you position a particular sculpture are probably as important considerations as the actual style of the artwork itself. Sometimes gardeners have a specific area that would welcome the adornment of an artwork, but it can take a long time to find the appropriate piece. At other times, just as with a plant in a garden centre or a painting in a gallery or an art exhibition, the sculpture is an impulse buy, as you seize the moment and acquire the piece just because you love it. Either way, there are myriad styles, sizes, materials and functions that will suit a range of gardens. To fully maximise the relationship between artwork and location, consider the style of your garden, the architecture of surrounding buildings and what the atmosphere of your private space is – these concerns may help you focus on the type of sculpture that is appropriate for your particular garden.

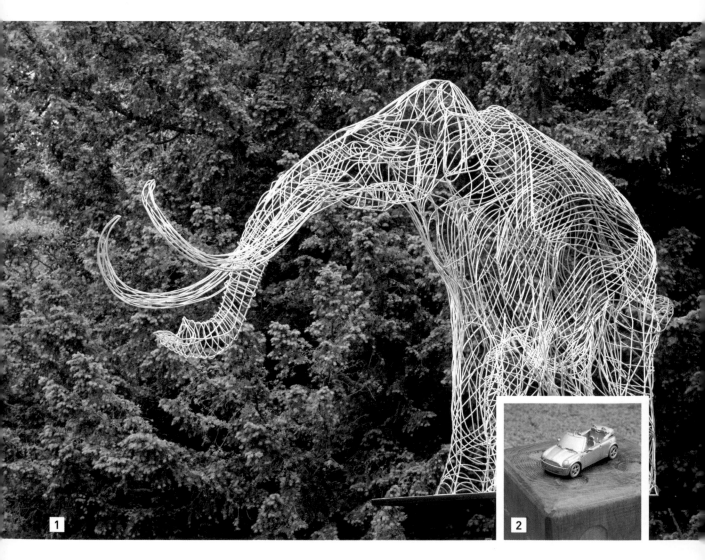

1

2

SCULPTURES IN FINE FOCUS

By including sculptures (large or small, temporary or permanent) in a garden you can add a welcome visual stimulus to an area.

1 An amazing mammoth sculpture, though not actually life-size, seems to be lurching forwards as it emerges from the trees behind. In doing so, it demonstrates not only the sublime composition of the artwork, but also how the backdrop of trees helps set the scene for dramatic effect.

2 This model of a Mini convertible on top of a wooden die is at the other end of the artwork scale. It makes playful reference to the garden's narrative, which is linked to a well-known family board game.

3 The magnificent horse's head has been plated together by the artist, giving it an industrial metallic feel. A thing of beauty for many, it is a bold display of artistic endeavour.

4 Taking cues from the way an art gallery would display its subjects inside a building, these three plinths are home to different sculptural artworks. Note how the white backing panels help show off the works to greater effect.

5 Although appearing much more understated, this metal keyhole design in fact has three roles: it acts as a piece of art in itself; it creates an entrance for the visitor to pass through into the garden; and it frames a view to the sculptural moon at the far end of the space.

6 An oversized daisy brings a sense of fun and humour to this design. Such creations boldly take their inspiration from nature and are then, often, best suited to 'natural' surroundings.

Sculpture for strong effect

So much of using a sculpture successfully depends on how the overall garden design is put together, and how the visitor is encouraged (or directed) to view the scene. Sometimes sculptures can make bold visual statements, overtly showing that they exist; at other times, they are much more subtle, partly hidden in foliage or maybe changing in texture or colour over time. It may sound unnerving, but putting a piece of artwork into the wrong location can be devastating – not only to the garden but also to the piece in question. For new gardens, it may be easier to start off with an artwork and then plant or decorate around it; for more mature gardens a chance gap in a hedge or among plants may warrant the creative addition. Either way, practical considerations such as how the piece is to be fixed to a secure base (especially in times of heavy rain, strong winds or against theft) are also important.

PURPOSE AND STYLE

Given appropriate forethought as to where the artwork is to be sited, the gardener's artistic intention can be well satisfied.

1 A brushed steel sculpture is beautifully enhanced by the surrounding metal pergola and numerous plants growing around it.

2 This fun, contemporary take on society in the 1980s has a dual purpose: as a visual sculpture and as a water feature. The planting softens the overall effect (but less so in winter owing to plant types).

3 Time for tea? Sometimes the intention of sculptures can be to raise a smile or reaction in the garden visitor, which is no bad thing.

4 A sculptural fern appears to be growing out of the *Muehlenbeckia*, and contrasts both in scale and material colour to great effect.

EXPERT TIP

Philip Nash
How to position a sculpture

❛ When considering where to site sculpture in a garden, decide whether you wish to create a focal point where your eye is drawn to pause on the piece before leading to the vista beyond, or if the focal point is to be the final destination. Is your sculpture to blend in with its surroundings or is it to stand out? And in that position will it match the surrounding style, be it classic, contemporary, natural or romantic? Look for a 'natural' place to set an artwork – one that feels right and best creates the effect you are seeking. For example, you may want the sculpture to be in a prominent position that will command attention, or you may prefer your garden visitors to discover an artwork placed off to the side (within a planted border). An artwork set in front of a wall or hedge will give it presence and/or provide a solid backdrop; if you don't have a suitable backdrop, consider creating a standalone panel or wall. Always light your artworks – illumination helps create atmosphere and drama. And, finally, don't clutter a garden with too many pieces, with too many focal points vying for attention. ❜

Sculpture can be challenging to site properly, but when forethought and consideration have been used it can achieve great visual drama – as this dry-stone sphere (and associated imprint within the wall) demonstrate.

Integrity in place

Whereas many pieces of garden art are bought as standalone additions to a garden, some schemes have a much more integrated approach – and Chelsea show gardens are prime examples of this. Their role and purpose are central to the design, bringing together a well-balanced and seamless relationship between planting, hard landscaping, spatial division, practical use and visual appeal. The role of the artwork can be as individual as the garden itself, but the intention should be that without that piece of art your garden would not be as successful as it could be. From wildlife homes to sculptural forms, and vertical finishes to contemporary statements, an integrated approach to artwork and garden-making can create a truly successful outside space.

1

2

DEFINED ROLES

Artwork, whether freestanding or supported, can be as integral to a garden as any other material.

1 Merging artistic and sustainable ideas with practical wildlife use, this vertical 'bug home' incorporates recycled materials, interesting shapes and a quirky overall style.

2 Three arched posts seem to leap out from the informal planting below, and thereby add movement and height to this space.

3 Walls and artwork merge in this unusual design of interconnecting and related circles and hoops, which bring a gratifying sense of flow.

4 These sculptural pineapple cones give focus and a sense of scale to this fine display of clipped topiary forms.

Full-on, vibrant colour reigns supreme here
The sculptural sun at the back of the space picks
up the planting in the foreground, especially the
blue-flowered lupins and yellow spires of
Verbascum, which visually link to the sun's rays.
**From Life to Life, A Garden for George, Yvonne
Innes, 2008**

Personalising space

One of the most fun aspects of garden-making is the personalisation of space, whether in terms of planting combinations, spatial division or how a place is decorated or adorned. The last can be easily and cost effectively achieved in a garden. Often, the placing of a simple sculpture, a combination of elements (such as a group of pots near a water feature) or an actual home-made artefact can be an artistic statement in its own right.

In so doing, the gardener is showing not only a creative side but also staking a visible claim to his/her territory, showing that the space in question belongs or relates to them. And it can be fun! Gardening should be about the personality of the owner coming through, representing unique journeys or historical endeavours. By combining sculpture and art with garden-making, a really personal space can be created.

UNUSUAL TOUCHES

Using local or relevant materials, a personal and specific piece of art can be produced.

1 More than 50 spade heads, new and old, were used to form this substantial sculpture in a garden – for evident reasons – named 'The Ace of Spades'.

2 Charming details such as a stone bead 'necklace' atop a rustic fence can bring bucket-loads of personality and interest to a tiny corner of a garden.

3 In this highly detailed piece of artwork, thousands of different-coloured gravel pieces have been laid in a path leading to a front door, so they recreate scenes from London. As the path is increasingly used, the designer anticipated that the gravel would be moved around and so slowly change the entire pictorial composition.

4 This attractive combination blends historical gardening tools with a contemporary, gridded backing. Together, they make an unusual but personal wall-hung sculpture.

3

EXPERT TIP

Philip Nash
Anchoring sculpture for safety and security

❛ Part of the joy with many pieces of artwork is the apparent 'ease' by which they arise from the ground, so ground fixing is essential. How you secure any piece of artwork in position is dependent on what you have bought or created: its size and material (or materials) will throw up unique challenges and demand specific logistical thought. Generally, though, pots and containers that are to stay in the same location for a long time (that is, not be moved for seasonal display) can be bolted to paving or concrete plinths by drilling a hole through each pot from inside and using a super-strength adhesive to secure it in place. Add weight with ballast to ensure the container really won't move – this not only reduces damage from wind rock but also helps deter any burglars from easily walking out with one of your prized pots. Sculptures (stone or cast pieces, timber or steel) can also be anchored to plinths or concrete pads but do not allow fixing points to be seen; such artworks are best avoided in areas where ball games take place or a high number of visitors may pass. Other products on the market are special anchors and subterranean chains that hold a sculpture in place, without causing visual disruption. If long grass is growing around the base, remember this will need maintaining; strimmers may damage any artwork, so hand cutting of the turf may be necessary. ❜

Lightweight home made artworks can be cleverly anchored to a gate or fence relatively easily, but bigger pieces of work will need considerably stronger fixings.

4

THE SAVILLS GARDEN

Clean lines, simple white walls and defined areas are all common design techniques in a house, but now increasingly so in a modern garden, too. Here, designer Philip Nixon has brought rigour and precision to a Chelsea garden: the structure and geometry of the garden allowed for your eye to go from one space to another without interruption, helped along with simple box hedges, waving grasses and punctuations of colour. Less, as is so often the case in garden design, was definitely more.

The brief stated that this design was to be 'a secluded section of a larger garden owned by a collector of abstract painting and sculpture'. As a result, the designer used the concept of picture framing (the white walls, right, and white frames, below) to great effect, not only showing off the content within the frame (just like a wall-hung picture) but also allowing the planting itself to be seen as a picture against a white backdrop. Other techniques such as low-lying, raised water beds gave the space reflection and added depth – again, just like a painter would employ in a piece of art. The real success of this garden, however, was the fact that it was a defined space – in other words, it stood well on its own, just like an average garden at home should.

CONSIDER ITS MAIN DESIGN FEATURES:

- white walls and hornbeam hedging edge the space;
- there is a clear progression down the garden, from the front to the back;
- there are areas to sit or stand in, allowing the visitor to take in the garden and its pieces of art;
- pools of water add movement, light and reflection;
- the planting mixes different textures of green with controlled but co-ordinated areas of flowering plants;
- white paint is used to lighten the overall feel of the space;
- containers give height to the horizontal plane;
- there is not too much ongoing maintenance needed (apart from a lot of hedge cutting).

1 Graceful *Stipa gigantea*, when viewed against the white painted panels behind, not only has its flowerheads brought into sharp focus but also creates shadows and shapes on the wall.

2 Simple square paving slabs, in grey basalt, were used to link with the grey walls. This made the white panels (with dark wood framing) stand out as much as possible. The slabs bring a lightness to this area in between hedging and planting and also act as a foil for the grey-slate columnar planters by the wall.

DESIGNER Philip Nixon

CONTRACTOR Landform Consultants Ltd

AWARD Gold

CATEGORY Show Garden, 2008

SPONSOR Savills plc

KEY WORDS formal; contemporary; refined; linear; frames

IN A SENTENCE... Looks easy to achieve, but needs an amazing amount of precision to be executed well.

3 More white panels provide consistency across the garden – a key design skill. Shadows, light and shapes thrown against the panels give the effect of a 'living sculpture' – shadows change throughout the day as light levels alter. Note also the canopy-raised tree, whose branches can be seen to great effect 'backlit' by the white wall.

4 Water is an essential element in a garden for many people, and this example shows just how to introduce it. The black-lined, raised pools, enclosed by tightly clipped box hedges, bring a sense of calm, and on brighter days (as here) give reflections of this outdoor space.

5 Box hedging is perennially popular with designers, due to the ease by which it can be shaped into more or less any form you want. Here, however, the designer has used them in a traditional shape, edging all planting beds or water features with rectangular 'boxes'. The result is a tightly controlled, simple effect.

6 With this flowery, willowy planting combination of foxgloves and young fennel leaves, the whole mood of this garden is softened. The dominance of the clipped box is substantially reduced, and a liveliness is created by the three-dimensional nature of the planting.

DESIGNER CREDITS

1997 **YVES ST LAURENT'S MARRAKECH GARDEN** • Designer: Madison Cox Sponsor: Yves St Laurent; 18

2000 **A CITY SPACE** • Designer: Mark Anthony Walker Sponsor: Cartier Ltd; 18

2001 **GARDEN FOR LEARNING** • Designer: Johnny Woodford, Cleve West; 23

2002 **KELLY'S CREEK** • Designer: Alison Wear, Miranda Melville

2003 **THE LACE AND TAPESTRY GARDEN** • Designer: Kay Yamada Sponsor: Barakura English Garden; 22

GARDEN FROM THE DESERT • Designer: Christopher Bradley-Hole Sponsor: His Highness Sheikh Zayed Bin Sultan al-Nahyan; 19

SHOW GARDENS 2004 THE MERRILL LYNCH GARDEN • Designer: Dan Pearson Studio Sponsor: Merrill Lynch

HORTUS CONCLUSUS • Designer: Christopher Bradley-Hole Sponsor: His Highness Shaikh Zayed Bin Sultan Al-Nahyan

LAURENT-PERRIER HARPERS & QUEEN GARDEN • Designer: Terence Conran, Nicola Lesbirel Sponsors: Laurent-Perrier, Harpers & Queen

THE SALVATION ARMY & BUILDBASE GARDEN – 'FROM DARKNESS TO LIGHT' • Designer: Julian Dowle (Julian Dowle Partnership) Sponsor: Buildbase

THE STONEMARKET BOAT RACE ANNIVERSARY GARDEN • Designer: Bunny Guinness Sponsor: Stonemarket

THE NATIONAL LOTTERY GARDEN – 'A COLOURFUL SUBURBAN EDEN' • Designer: Diarmuid Gavin Sponsor: The National Lottery

THE KNIGHTSBRIDGE URBAN RENAISSANCE GARDEN • Designer: Phil Jaffa (Scape Design Associates) in association with Patrick Collins Sponsor: The Knightsbridge Development; 120 (b); 194 (l)

LIFE GARDEN • Designer: Jane Hudson, Erik De Maeijer Sponsor: Thompson Landscapes; 124 (tl), 196 (cl)

THE HADDONSTONE KNOT GARDEN • Designer: Simon Scott Sponsor: Haddonstone Ltd

FLEMINGS NURSERIES AUSTRALIAN INSPIRATION • Designer: Jim Fogarty (Jim Fogarty Design Pty Ltd) Sponsor: Flemings Nurseries

THE DAIHATSU GREEN GARDEN • Designer: The Burntwood School Sponsor: Daihatsu Cars

WILLIAM TURNER GARDEN • Designers: Casella Stanger, Chris Davis Sponsors: Northumberland Strategic Partnership, Morpeth Town Council, Heritage Lottery Fund, Casella Stanger, Hellens

THE GARDMAN WILD BIRD GARDEN • Designer: David Domoney Sponsor: Gardman Ltd

100% PURE NEW ZEALAND ORA – GARDEN OF WELL-BEING • Designers: Kim Jarrett, Trish Waugh, Lyonel Grant, Doug Waugh, Tina Hart, Brian Massey Sponsor: Tourism New Zealand

THE PAVESTONE GARDEN • Designer: Geoffrey Whiten Sponsor: Pavestone (UK) Ltd in association with Essential Water Garden Magazine; 42 (b)

THE 4HEAD GARDEN – FROM MERLIN TO MEDICINE • Designer: Marney Hall, Sponsor: 4head

THE PLANT HUNTERS • Designers: Mike Baldwin, Gill Thomas Sponsor: Bradstone

FROM FREEDOM TO FUTURE • Designer: Park & Countryside Landscape Architects (Leeds City Council) Sponsor: Leeds City Council, with assistance from Thorpe Park Leeds and Munro K

THE JAPANESE WAY • Designer: Maureen Busby Garden Designs Sponsors: CED, Herons Bonsai, Coblands, Travis Perkins

HOPE • Designers: Staff and prisoners from HMP Leyhill Sponsor: Gem Horticulture

THE WOOLWORTHS GARDEN • Designers: Graduates from The Pickard School of Garden Design Sponsor: Woolworths

SHOW GARDENS 2005

MERRILL LYNCH GARDEN • Designer: Andy Sturgeon (Andy Sturgeon Garden Design) Sponsor: Merrill Lynch; 108; 139 (t); 210-211

IN THE GROVE • Designer: Christopher Bradley-Hole Sponsor: His late Highness Shaikh Zayed bin Sultan Al-Nahyan; 148-149

LAURENT-PERRIER GARDEN • Designer: Tom Stuart-Smith Landscape Design Sponsors: Laurent-Perrier (UK) Ltd, Trentham Leisure Ltd; 73 (bl)

THE ECOVER CHELSEA PENSIONERS' GARDEN • Designer: Julian Dowle (Julian Dowle Partnership) Sponsor: Ecover

THE PEACE GARDEN • Designer: Sir Terence Conran (Conran & Partners) Sponsor: Big Lottery Fund; 99 (l)

HANOVER QUAY GARDEN • Designer: Diarmuid Gavin Sponsors: Park

Developments Ltd and John Sisk & Son Ltd, Marshalls, Westland Horticulture, Unwins Seeds, Marian Finucane Show; 95 (cr)

THE TRAILFINDERS RECYCLED GARDEN • Designer: Chris Beardshaw Ltd Sponsor: Trailfinders; 128-129; 142 (r)

THE FETZER WINE GARDEN • Designer: Kate Frey Sponsor: Brown-Forman Wines; 69 (bl); 112

THE CANCER RESEARCH UK GARDEN • Designers: Jane Hudson & Erik De Maeijer Sponsor: Private donor; 31 (b); 117 (tl)

FLEMING'S NURSERIES FLOAT • Designer: Jack Merlo (Jack Merlo Design) Sponsor: Fleming's Nurseries; 52 (b); 107 (tr)

BOREAL FOREST GARDEN • Designer: Landlab Sponsors: Taiga Rescue Network, Lorberg Baumschulerzeugnisse, United Utilities, Laurieston Hall Community, Landlab; 161 (tr and br)

MOAT & CASTLE ECO-GARDEN • Designers: Ellen Mary Fenton & Neil Malachy Black Sponsor: National Savings and Investments

SAVILLS GARDEN: THE GRAND TOUR • Designer: Clare Agnew Sponsor: Savills in association with After the Antique; 109 (br)

THE 4HEAD GARDEN • Designer: Marney Hall Sponsor: 4head; 117 (tr)

BRADSTONE SPRING GARDEN • Designer: Alan Sargent Sponsor: Bradstone

THE WILDLIFE TRUSTS LUSH GARDEN • Designer: Stephen Hall Sponsor: Lush UK; 97 (tr); 166 (tl)

THE REAL RUBBISH GARDEN • Designer: Claire Whitehouse Sponsor: SITA Environmental Trust; 114-115; 146

THE FISHERMAN'S GARDEN • Designers: Geoffrey Whiten, Josh Whiten Sponsor: Pavestone; 114-115; 146

THE SPIRAL GARDEN • Designer: Carol Smith Sponsors: M&M Timber, Marshalls, Osmose, Steve Cooper, Sugarbrook Nurseries, Colin Smith Electrical, AC Electrical, Buildbase, Topglass, University of Gloucestershire, Worcester Aquatics

CHIC GARDENS THE GALLERY OUTSIDE • Designer: Philip Nixon, Marcus Barnett; 147 (br)

THE ROALD DAHL FOUNDATION CHOCOLATE GARDEN • Designer: Landscape Management Services / Home Group Sponsors: Home Group, Warner Bros; 142 (l)

COURTYARD GARDENS THE PHILOSOPHER'S GARDEN • Designer: Andrew Loudon Sponsor: SWS UK Ltd; 209 (r)

THE CUMBRIAN FELLSIDE GARDEN • Designer: Kim Wilde, Richard Lucas Sponsors: Wyevale Garden Centres plc, The World of Beatrix Potter, Cumbria Tourist Board, Holker Hall and Gardens; 215

SIMON'S GARDEN WITH VA VA VROOM • Designer: Scenic Blue Design Team; 147 (tr); 118 (tr)

CITY GARDEN REFLECTIONS • Designer: David Domoney Sponsor: The Sunday Mirror; 62-63; 133 (tr)

SHOW GARDENS 2006

SAGA INSURANCE GARDEN • Designer: Cleve West Sponsor: Saga Insurance; 111 (b)

THE SAVILLS GARDEN • Designers: Marcus Barnett, Philip Nixon Sponsor: Savills plc; 34-35; 61 (tl); 77 (tl); 207 (b); 53 (tr)

LAURENT-PERRIER GARDEN • Designer: Jinny Blom (Jinny Blom Ltd) Sponsor: Laurent-Perrier (UK) Ltd; 56 (tl)

THE DAILY TELEGRAPH GARDEN • Designer: Tom Stuart-Smith Sponsor: The Daily Telegraph; 52-53; 111 (tr); 38 (br); 70

THE 100% PURE NEW ZEALAND GARDEN • Designer: Xanthe White Sponsor: Tourism New Zealand supported by Air New Zealand, Tourism Auckland, Tailor Made Travel, Titan HiTours; 7 (l); 105 (b); 121; 124 (bl); 205 (c); 209 (l)

WALKING BAREFOOT WITH BRADSTONE • Designer: Sarah Eberle in collaboration with Andrew Herring Sponsor: Bradstone; 48-49; 89 (tr)

BARNSLEY HOUSE SPA GARDEN • Designer: Stephen Woodhams (Woodhams Ltd) Sponsor: Barnsley House; 8-9

THE CANCER RESEARCH UK GARDEN • Designer: Andy Sturgeon Sponsor: Private donor; 117 (b), 94

THE 4HEAD GARDEN OF DREAMS • Designers: Marney Hall, Heather Yarrow Sponsor: 4head; 117 (b)

RAVINE GARDEN: GIFT OF THE GLACIER • Designer: Catharina Malmberg-Snodgrass (CMS Design Associates) Sponsor: Lake Forest Garden Club

FLEMING'S NURSERIES AUSTRALIAN GARDEN PRESENTED BY TRAILFINDERS • Designer: Dean Herald Sponsors: Fleming's Nurseries, Trailfinders; 90 (t); 100-101; 124 (tr); 133 (b)

THE HALIFAX GARDEN – 'THESE FOUR WALLS' • Designer: Stuart Perry Consultants Sponsor: Halifax plc; 17; 91 (l); 120 (tl); 122-123

THE ROCKWOOL GARDEN ROOM • Designer: Barry Mayled Sponsor: Rockwool Ltd

LEEDS CITY COUNCIL GARDEN • Designer: Leeds City Council – Parks &

Countryside Service **Sponsor:** Munroe K
GARDENAFRICA • **Designer:** Alan Capper (Kent Design) in partnership with Ross Allan Designs **Sponsor:** UK based charitable trusts; 6 (bl)
THE PAVESTONE GARDEN (A Garden of Tranquillity) • **Designer:** Geoffrey Whiten **Sponsor:** Pavestone UK Ltd
THE CHRIS BEARDSHAW WORMCAST GARDEN – 'GROWING FOR LIFE' AT BOVERIDGE HOUSE • **Designer:** Chris Beardshaw **Sponsor:** The Wormcast Company Ltd
THE JURASSIC COAST GARDEN • **Designer:** Nick Williams-Ellis **Sponsors:** Jurassic Coast Dorset & East Devon Heritage Site, Minster Joinery, Landers Quarries
GORILLA GARDEN • **Designer:** Graham Pockett **Sponsor:** Zoological Society of London; 95 (cl)

SHOW GARDENS 2007
THE AMNESTY INTERNATIONAL GARDEN FOR HUMAN RIGHTS • **Designers:** Paula Ryan, Artillery Architecture & Interior Design; 67 (b)
LLOYDS TSB GARDEN • **Designer:** Trevor Tooth **Sponsor:** Lloyds TSB
THE FETZER SUSTAINABLE WINERY GARDEN • **Designer:** Kate Frey **Sponsor:** Fetzer Vineyards; 164 (b)
SCENT OF A ROMAN • **Designer:** Leeds City Council – Parks & Countryside Service **Sponsors:** Thorpe Park Developments Ltd, Haddonstone Ltd
THE MARSHALL'S SUSTAINABILITY GARDEN • **Designer:** Scenic Blue Design Team **Sponsor:** Marshalls plc; 135 (b); 141 (r); 170-171
THE SAVILLS GARDEN • **Designer:** Marcus Barnett, Philip Nixon **Sponsor:** Savills plc; 109 (t)
LAURENT-PERRIER GARDEN • **Designer:** Jinny Blom (Jinny Blom Ltd) **Sponsor:** Laurent-Perrier (UK) Ltd; 46-47
THE DAILY TELEGRAPH GARDEN • **Designers:** Isabelle Van Groeningen, Gabriella Pape, artist Simon Packard **Sponsor:** Telegraph Media Group; 51; 76-77, 208 (tl)
THE CHRIS BEARDSHAW GARDEN IN ASSOCIATION WITH BUILDBASE • **Designer:** Chris Beardshaw **Sponsor:** Buildbase; 96 (t), 184 (l)
CANCER RESEARCH UK GARDEN • **Designer:** Andy Sturgeon Garden Design Ltd; 94 (t and br); 150-151
THE FORTNUM & MASON GARDEN • **Designer:** Robert Myers Associates **Sponsor:** Fortnum & Mason; 71 (b); 74 (tc); 119 (t); 160-161 (b)
600 DAYS WITH BRADSTONE • **Designer:** Sarah Eberle **Sponsor:** Bradstone; 6 (cl); 43 (r); 72 (r); 90 (b); 116 (br); 136 (b); 169 (t)
THE WESTLAND GARDEN • **Designers:** Diarmuid Gavin, Stephen Reilly **Sponsor:** Westland Horticulture Ltd; 82-83; 85 (c); 97 (b)
A TRIBUTE TO LINNAEUS • **Designer:** Ulf Nordfjell (Stockholm) **Sponsors:** The National Linnaeus Tercentenary Committee (Stockholm), Axel & Margaret Ax: son Johnson Foundation, The Bank of Sweden Tercentenary Foundation, The Sten A Olsson Foundation for Research & Culture; 12 (b); 45 (l); 54 (t); 139 (b); 143 (l)
FLEMING'S & TRAILFINDERS AUSTRALIAN GARDEN • **Designer:** Mark Browning (Cycas Landscape Design) **Sponsors:** Fleming's Nurseries, Trailfinders
THROUGH THE MOONGATE • **Designer:** Lesley Bremness (East West Garden Design), **Sponsors:** Royal Bank of Scotland Group, Bank of China; 45 (b); 85 (cr); 112 (inset)
THE THOMAS TELFORD TOLL HOUSE GARDEN • **Designers:** Michael Vout, Chris Jones **Sponsors:** Ironbridge Gorge Museum Trust, Harper Adams University College, P&W Maintenance Contracting Ltd, British Wildflower Plants, Telford & Wrekin Services Ltd, Dingle Nurseries, Shropshire Stone & Granite Ltd, Banbury Innovations – GRP products, Craven Dunnill Jackfield Ltd, Wellington Town Partnership.
THE BRETT LANDSCAPING GARDEN – RELATIONSHIPS • **Designer:** Geoffrey Whiten **Sponsor:** Brett Landscaping and Building Products
THE HASMEAD SAND & ICE GARDEN • **Designer:** Linda Bush **Sponsor:** Hasmead plc; 141 (l)
CHETWOODS GARDEN • **Designer:** Laurie Chetwood, Patrick Collins, 194 (r)
CHIC GARDEN **THE CHILDREN'S SOCIETY LUST FOR LIFE GARDEN** • **Designer:** Angus Thompson; 116 (tr)
CITY GARDEN **A CITY HAVEN COURTYARD** • **Designer:** Harpak design; 14-15; 124 (br)
REALISTIC RETREAT • **Designer:** Adam Frost; 125 (l)
COURTYARD GARDEN **CAF GIVING GARDEN 'WHERE THE WILD THINGS ARE'** • **Designer:** Tiggy Salt, Green Ink Gardens Ltd; 20
THE OLD GATE • **Designer:** Adam Woolcott, Jonathan Smith **Sponsors:** Croudace Homes, Langthorns Plantery, Cox's Architectural Salvage; 154-155; 176-177
TUFA TEA • **Designer:** Kati Crome; 137
SHINGLESEA • **Designer:** Chris O'Donoghue **Sponsor:** Robert Patch Furniture, 1066 Country, Merriments Gardens, Travis Perkins, John Jempson & Son; 44 (l); 69 (t); 155 (t); 214 (r)

CAPEL MANOR COLLEGE, CAPEL MANOR DESIGN • 205 (br)
CONTINUOUS LEARNING • Writtle College; 158 (t)
CLAPTON PARK PARK MANAGEMENT ORGANISATION/ GRASS ROOF COMPANY • 164 (t)
KIRSTENBOSCH • 140 (l)

SHOW GARDENS 2008
ELEVATIONS • **Designer:** Philip Nash (Philip Nash Designs) **Sponsor:** Gavin Jones Ltd, Dupont™ Corian ®, Philip Nash Design Ltd; 58-59; 50 (br); 110 (l)
SUMMER SOLSTICE • **Designers:** del buono Gazerwitz, Spencer Fung Architects; **Sponsor:** Daylesford Organic; 68 (r); 57 (tr); 186-187
OCEAN TO A GARDEN • **Designer:** Paul Cooper **Sponsors:** Testi Fratelli srl, H2O plc
THE LARGEST ROOM IN THE HOUSE • **Designer:** Denise Preston **Sponsors:** GMI Property Company Ltd, The Royal British Legion, Toc H; 04 (c); 57 (b)
THE MARSHALLS GARDEN THAT KIDS REALLY WANT! • **Designers:** Marshalls Gardens & Driveways, Ian Dexter **Sponsor:** Marshalls plc; 95 (b); 137 (l); 33
THE BUPA GARDEN • **Designer:** Cleve West **Sponsor:** Bupa; 64-65; 54 (bl)
I DREAM, I SEEK MY GARDEN • **Designer:** Shao Fan **Sponsors:** KT Wong Charitable Trust, De Beers, 15
THE SAVILLS GARDEN • **Designer:** Philip Nixon **Sponsor:** Savills plc; 54 (r); 94 (bl); 216-217
THE DAILY TELEGRAPH GARDEN • **Designer:** Arabella Lennox-Boyd **Sponsor:** The Daily Telegraph; 126-127
THE LAURENT-PERRIER GARDEN • **Designer:** Tom Stuart-Smith; 39; 78-79; 147 (tl)
CANCER RESEARCH UK GARDEN • **Designer:** Andy Sturgeon Garden Design Ltd; 2; 135 (t)
THE LLOYDS TSB GARDEN • **Designer:** Trevor Tooth; 38 (c); 40-41; 55 (l); 69 (tr); 120 (r); 139 (cl)
A CADOGAN GARDEN • **Designer:** Robert Myers **Sponsor:** Cadogan Estates Ltd; 12 (t); 32 (c); 39 (b and r); 60; 82 (b)
THE OCEÂNICO GARDEN • **Designers:** Diarmuid Gavin, Sir Terence Conran **Sponsor:** The Oceânico Group; 31 (tr); 43 (l); 66-67; 198-199; 200-201
FROM LIFE TO LIFE, A GARDEN FOR GEORGE • **Designer:** Yvonne Innes **Sponsors:** The Material World Charitable Foundation, Harrisongs Ltd; 140 (r); 212-213
FLEMING'S & TRAILFINDERS AUSTRALIAN GARDEN presented by Melbourne, Victoria • **Designer:** Jamie Durie (Patio Landscape Architecture & Design) **Sponsors:** Fleming's Nurseries, Trailfinders; 92-93; 117 (cr); 136 (t)
THE QVC GARDEN • **Designer:** Wynniatt-Husey Clarke Ltd **Sponsor:** QVC; 32 (bl); 33 (l); 72 (l); 85 (b)
THE REFLECTIVE GARDEN • **Designer:** Clare Agnew Design **Sponsor:** Ruffer LLP; 39 (tl); 85 (b)
NORTH EAST ENGLAND @ HOME GARDEN • **Designers:** Penny Denoon, John Carmichael **Sponsors:** Home Group Ltd, One NorthEast; 180 (l)
REAL LIFE BY BRETT • **Designer:** Geoff Whiten **Sponsors:** Brett Landscaping and Building Products; 74 (tl); 96 (b); 118 (tl)
GARDEN IN THE SILVER MOONLIGHT • **Designers:** Haruko Seki, Makoto Saito (add.locus architects) **Sponsors:** Royal Palm Residences Seychelles, Urban Regenerate Association of Niigata, The Great Britain Sasakawa Foundation; 109 (b) **Designer:** Gabriel Ash; 177 (tr)
URBAN GARDEN **THE SKY AT NIGHT** • **Designer:** Barry Mayled (Homes & Gardens Ltd.) **Sponsors:** Acorn Gardens, Euroclad Ltd., Hopkins Law LLP, Eurobond Ltd, Dudley's Ltd; 85 (t)
MIDORINO TOBIRA – THE GREEN DOOR • **Designer:** Kazuyuki Ishihara **Sponsor:** Oshhima Shipbuilding Group, AOA Corporation Ltd; 45 (r)
THE LK BENNETT GARDEN • **Designer:** Rachel de Thame; 56 (b l); 133 (br)
THE CHILDREN'S SOCIETY GARDEN • **Designer:** Mark Gregory; 138 (b); 166 (tr)
THE PEMBERTON GREENISH RECESS GARDEN • **Designer:** Paul Hensey with Knoll Gardens **Sponsor:** Pemberton Greenish; 26 (b); 33 (b); 53 (b); 91 r; 125 (tr); 132-133
TEMPEST IN A TEAPOT • **Designer:** Thomas Hoblyn Garden Design Ltd **Sponsor:** Foreign & Colonial Investment Trust; 32 (r); 111 (tl)
COURTYARD GARDEN **THE DORSET CEREALS EDIBLE PLAYGROUND** • **Designer:** Nick Williams; 181 (l); 182 (bl); 183 r; 184 (b)
THE SIMMONS & SIMMONS GARDEN: A JOURNEY TO WORK • **Designer:** Growing Ambition **Sponsors:** Simmons & Simmons; 97 (tl)
SPANA'S COURTYARD GARDEN • **Designer:** Chris O'Donoghue **Sponsor:** SPANA 83 (t)
THE SHETLAND CROFT HOUSE GARDEN • **Designer:** Sue Hayward **Sponsors:** Motor Neurone Disease; 111 (bl)
SAIL FOR GOLD • Hilliers; 96 (tr)
CHRISTOPHER LISNEY • Garden Sculpture; 208 (cr)

SHOW GARDENS 2009

THE CANARY ISLANDS SPA GARDEN • Designers: David Cubero & James Wong Sponsor: Canary Islands Tourist Board; 81 (t); 59 (bc)

ECHOES OF JAPAN IN AN ENGLISH GARDEN • Designer: Kay Yamada Sponsors: Barakura English Garden, TV Kanagawa Inc, Asahi Breweries Ltd, All Nippon Airways Co Ltd, Daikanen; 105 (t); 195 (cr)

THE QVC GARDEN • Designer: Adam Frost Sponsor: QVC; 125 (b)

FUTURE NATURE • Designers: Adrian Hallam, Chris Arrowsmith, Nigel Dunnett Sponsors: Yorkshire Water, University of Sheffield Alumni Fund, Green City Initiative, Buro Happold; 68 (l); 159; 172-173; 210 (l)

THE MARSHALLS LIVING STREET • Designer: Ian Dexter (Marshalls) Sponsor: Marshalls plc; 26 (t); 36 (r); 15 (bl); 157 (bl); 167 (b)

THE FOREIGN & COLONIAL INVESTMENT'S GARDEN • Designer: Thomas Hoblyn Sponsor: Foreign & Colonial Investment Trust; 106-107 (t); 113 (b)

THE DAILY TELEGRAPH GARDEN • Designer: Ulf Nordfjell Sponsor: The Daily Telegraph; 16; 61 (b); 66 (l); 67 (t);74 (br);83 (b)

THE LAURENT-PERRIER GARDEN • Designer: Luciano Giubbilei Sponsor: Champagne Laurent-Perrier; 24-25; 63 (r); 196 (r)

THE CANCER RESEARCH UK GARDEN • Designer: Robert Myers Sponsor: Cancer Research UK; 27; 119 (b); 211 (t)

THE KEY • Designer: Paul Stone Sponsors: Homes and Communities Agency, Communities and Local Government, London Employer Accord; 165 (l and br); 167 (tl); 203 (t)

THE HESCO GARDEN • Designer: Leeds City Council Sponsor: HESCO Bastion Ltd; 113 (t); 155 (b)

THE QUILTED VELVET GARDEN • Designer: Tony Smith Sponsor: Quilted Velvet; 90 (lm)

PERFUME GARDEN • Designers: Laurie Chetwood & Patrick Collins Sponsors: Gazeley, P&G Prestige Products and Chetwoods Architects

URBAN GARDENS THE WITAN WISDOM GARDEN • Designer: Nicholas Dexter; Sponsor: Witan Investment Trust; 37 (b); 86-87

ECO CHIC • Designers: Kate Gould • Sponsor: Helios; 88 (r); 102-103; 143 (r); 28 (b); 37 (f)

THE CHILDREN'S SOCIETY GARDEN • Designer: Mark Gregory; 98 (tl and br); 118 (b); 179 (bl); 188; 192 (tl); 195 (tl)

CREDIT CRUNCH: THE OVERDRAWN ARTIST'S GARDEN • Designer: Sarah Eberle; 215 (t and bl)

CREDIT CRUNCH: THE OFF-SHORE GARDEN • Designer: Sarah Eberle; 44 (r)

CREDIT CRUNCH: THE BANKER'SGARDEN • Designer: Sarah Eberle; 206

NATURE ASCENDING • Designers: Jane Broadbank, Angus Thompson; 10-11 (tc); 29 (b);157 (t); 161 (tl and cl);162-163

1984 • Designer: Anthony Cox, Chris Gutteridge, Jon Owens; 158 (b); 208 (b)

THE PSI NURSERY GARDEN • Designer: Jamie Dunstan Sponsor: PSI Nursery; 50 (b); 95 (t)

THE FENCHURCH GARDEN • Designer: Paul Hensey Sponsor: Fenchurch Advisory Partners; 28-29;157 (br)

THE MODERN ROCK GARDEN • Designer: Tomoko Osonoe Sponsor: Tecnoplan Co Ltd; 31 (l); 72 (tl)

A JAPANESE TRANQUIL RETREAT • Designer: Takumi Awai; 195 (tr)

THE ACE OF SPADES • Designer: David Domoney; 98 (tr); 165 (tr); 214 (l);

COURTYARD GARDEN TIME TO THINK, SPACE TO BREATHE • Designers: Tony Davy, Mike Roberts, Warwickshire College; 166 (b)

FENLAND ALCHEMIST GARDEN • Designers: Jane Besser, Stephen Hall; 21

POTTERING IN NORTH CUMBRIA • Designers: Stephen Hall, Jane Besset; 160 (t)

DEMELZA • Designer: Jo Thompson; 156

FRESHLY PREPARED BY ARALIA • Designer: Patrica Fox (Aralia Garden Design); Sponsors: Pawley & Malyon, Heather Barnes, Attwater & Liell; 184 (tr); 185 (r); 182 (c)

GENERATION GARDENS RANELAGH SCHOOL LEARNING TO GROW • Designers: Mary Payne, Jon Wheatley in partnership with Ranelagh School; 178

THE WIDOW'S GARDEN • Garden Design Centre at Scotsdale; 42 (t)

OTHER THE SCULPTURE PARK, Jumps Road, Churt, Farnham, Surrey; 206

ARCHITECTURAL HERITAGE, Horse of the Moon Artist: Nic Fiddian Green; 207

MARSTON AND LANZINGER; 176; 182-183

A PLANTSMAN'S PALETTE' Roger Platts Garden Design and Nurseries; 56 (r); 62 (t); 84 (t)

THOMPSON'S GALLERY, (in association with Janet Macleod); 205 (t)

INDEX

Figures in *italics* indicate captions.

A

Acer palmatum 103
Achillea 71
acrylics 143
Agapanthus 58
Agave americana 69
  'Mediopicta alba' 58
air temperature 166
Al-Nahyan, His late Highness Shaikh Zayed bin Sultan 149
Alchemilla mollis 56, 62, 167
algae 113
Allium 52, 53, 71, 120, 160
alliums 200, 201
allotment waiting lists 176
alpine strawberries 169
aluminium, soda-blasted 135
amphibians 113
Anethum graveolens (dill) 185
annuals 68, 168
Aponogeton distachyos (water hawthorn) 110
apple tree 181
  Aquilegia 53
  chrysantha 'Yellow Queen' 77
Arabic style 18, *18*, 22
arboreta 82
arches 28
architectural planting 132
Ark Design Management 172, 173
Armeria 167
Arrowsmith, Chris 172, 173
art in the garden 202-17
  anchoring sculpture for safety and security 215, *215*
  case study 216, 216-17
  defined roles 211
  how to position a sculpture 209, *209*
  integrity in place 210, *210*
  location, location 206
  personalising space 214, *214*
  sculpture for strong effect 208, *208*
  sculptures in fine focus 207
Artemisia 56
  dracunculus (French tarragon) 179
Asarum europaeum 79
Astelia chathamica 54
astrantias 47, 79
awnings 82, 99

B

balconies 143, 169
balustrades 143
bamboos 127, 148, 149
barbccucs 83
Barnett, Marcus 145
bay 74
beans 183
Beardshaw, Chris 128, 129
bedding plants 56, 68, 141
bees 21, 155, 160
  bee 'hotel' 160
benches 48, 76, 84, *84*, 88, 88, 89, 103, 132, 139, 159, 181

Betula (birch) 33
  utilis (white-stemmed birch) 173
bicycles 99
biker theme 99
biodiversity 97, 155, 163, 164
birch (Betula) 33, 35, 54, 61, 194
  white-stemmed (Betula utilis) 173
bird feeders 160
bird's foot trefoil (Lotus corniculatus) 169
birds, nesting 157
Blom, Jinny 28, 46, 47
blueberries 177
boardwalk, timber 41, 148
boats 17, 21
bonsai 79
Bougainvillea 18
boulders 37, 67
bound rope-house 160
Boveridge House, Dorset 128, 129
bowls 58
box (Buxus) 22, 25, 29, 54, 55, 56, 60, 61, 67, 73, 76, 79, 82, 100, 217
Bradley-Hole, Christopher 148, 149
Bradstone garden 48, 48-9
Brambles Garden Landscapes 187
Brassica juncea (mustard) 185
bricks 28, 39, 43, 171
Brockbank, Jane 163, 213
bronze 205
Brookes, John 100, 190
Brundtland Commission 154
Brussels sprouts 176-7
'bug home' 211
Building Regulations: 'Part P' 195
bulbs 63, 63, 68, 168
Bupa Garden, Cleve West (2008) 65
busy Lizzies 91
Buxus (box) 55, 56, 61, 67, 73, 79

C

cabbages 177, 187
cacti 18, 137
Calendula 72
campanulas 76
Cancer Research UK Garden 150, 150-51
candles 99, 99
Canna 55
car windscreen 165
cardoons 151, 181, 187
case studies
  Bradstone garden 48, 48-9
  Cancer Research UK Garden 150, 150-51
  Chris Beardshaw Wormcast Garden 'Growing for Life' at Boveridge House 128, 128-9
  Daily Telegraph garden 76, 76-7
  Eco Chic 102, 102-3
  Fleming's & Trailfunders Australian Garden 93, 100, 100-101
  Future Nature 172, 172-3
  In the grove 148, 149
  Laurent-Perrier garden 46, 46-7, 78, 78-9
  Marshalls' Sustainability Garden 170, 171
  Oceânico Garden 199, 200, 200-201

Savills Garden 218, 218-19
  Summer Solstice 186, 186-7
  The *Daily Telegraph* garden 126, 127
catalpa 129
CDs, recycled 29
cedar 145
  Western red 137, 139
chairs 43, 84, 85, 95
  'daisy'-like seats 85
  deckchairs 141
  moulded 85
chamomile 139
Chelsea pensioners 113
children 177, 184
Chinese tea houses 94
chives 181, 187
Chris Beardshaw Wormcast Garden
  'Growing for Life' at Boveridge
  House 128, 129
chrysanthemums 68
Cirsium rivulare 'Atropurpureum' 55, 155
Cistus (sun roses) 56
citrus plants 184
classic style 18, 21
Clematis 160
climate change 58, 83, 141, 156, 169,
  172
climbers 76, 168
cloud pruning 73, 73, 78, 78, 79, 79
cobbles 31, 44
colanders 177, 184
colour
  colour-themed planting 62, 62, 76
  coloured materials 140, 141
  ribbons of 164
columns, concrete 49
composting 154, 164
concrete 28, 38, 43, 48, 49, 89, 171, 215
  manufacturing 157
conifers 18, 68
Conran, Sir Terence 199, 200, 201
containers 29, 72, 72, 73, 74, 79, 110,
  140, 215, 216
  growing produce in 184-5, 184
  mosaic 141
  and recycling 154, 158
  terracotta 18
contemporary style 17-18, 17, 22
conversation pit 91, 91
Convolvulus cneorum 74
cookers 83
copper beech 193
Cordyline 58
corms 63
corn poppy (*Papaver rhoeas*) 56
Cornus controversa 151
cos lettuces 181
cottage gardens 52, 54, 54, 113
cow parsley (*Anthriscus sylvestris*
  'Ravenswing') 56
cowslip (*Primula veris*) 169
Craddock, Tony 193, 195, 196-7
cress 184
Crocus.co.uk 47, 77, 79, 127
cupboards, outdoor 99, 166
cushions 85, 91, 91, 99, 100, 101
Cycas revoluta 58
cypresses 18

D
daffodils 52
Dahlia 142
dahlias 52-3
Daily Telegraph garden 76, 76-7, 126, 127
daisy 'flowers', metal mesh 200, 200
Davies, Iestyn 115, 117
day beds 90, 91
Daylesford Organic 187
deckchairs 141
decking 93, 95, 109, 139
  glass 37
  wooden 28, 28, 38, 107, 113, 137,
  137, 145, 149
del Buono, Tommaso 187
del Buono Gazerwitz 186
delphiniums 76
Dexter, Nicholas 87
Dianthus 169
  carthusianorum 69
Digitalis 54, 71, 129
dill (*Anethum graveolens*) 185
dining areas 48
doors 28
dovecote 99
downlighting 196
drainpipes 172
drought 159
drought-tolerant planting 58, 58, 69,
  69, 154
Dunnett, Nigel 69, 159, 169, 172, 173
Durie, Jamie 93

E
earth-and-rubble bank 170, 171
Eberle, Sarah 28, 48, 49
Echeveria species 58, 74
Eco Chic garden 102, 102-3
education 177
electricity, electricians 106, 194, 195,
  195, 196, 200
entrances 28, 44, 44, 45
environment 155, 166, 170, 172
environmental awareness 156
Erodium manescavii 69, 169
Eruca vesicaria subsp. *sativa* (salad
  rocket) 185
Ethical Trading Initiative Base Code 170
Euonymus 72
evergreens 68
Ewing, Andrew 113, 118-19
extensions, small 169

F
fairy lights 99, 99
feeding 72
fencing 28, 36, 138, 142
  derelict fence 113
  iron railings 28, 36, 36
  reused timber 36
  rustic 44, 110
  wooden posts 36
fennel 217
  bronze 181
ferns 169
fertilisers 154, 185
Festuca gautieri 66
firepits 91, 133

fireplaces, outdoor 100, 101, 187
Fleming's & Trailfinders Australian
  Garden (2008) 93, 100, 100-101
Fleming's Nurseries of Australia 83
flint, knapped 145
flood risk 159
flooring
  reinforced glass 87, 143
  terracotta 18
Foerster, Karl 76, 77
'food miles' 165, 177, 178
formal style 22, 22, 109
fountains 106, 128, 196
foxgloves (*Digitalis*) 45, 129, 142, 217
French tarragon (*Artemisia dracunculus*)
  179
front gardens 157
Frost, Adam 30-31, 43
fruit 99, 154, 176, 176, 177, 178, 183,
  186
Future Nature 172, 172-3

G
gabions 31, 134, 135, 141, 147, 155, 170,
  171
gallery, outside 147
garages 169
Garden Builders, The 103
garden features 82
garden/outdoor rooms 48, 49, 82, 82,
  97, 100, 141, 192
gardening tools, historical 214
gates 28, 187
  moon gate 28, 45, 46, 47
  solar 46, 46
Gaura lindheimeri 69
Gavin, Diarmuid 28, 199, 200, 201
gazebos 128
Gazerwitz, Paul 187
Geranium phaeum 'Album' 71
Geum 62
geums 77
glass 13, 29, 143
  car windscreen 165
  decking 37
  flooring 87, 101
  panels 143
  pebbles 118
  screens 37, 102
  sculpture 110, 117, 125, 205
  tiles 195
glass rooms 94
Gould, Kate 102, 103
gourds 186
granite 66, 67
grass, and wildlife 68, 160
grasses 46, 47, 53, 55, 63, 77, 148
grassland, chalk or limestone 169
gravel 116, 204, 214
greenhouses 82
'grey water' reuse 102, 159, 170
ground water levels 154
groundcover plants 72
'growing your own' (GYO) 176, 178, 182
Guinness, Bunny 91, 99
Gunnera manicata 127

H
Halifax Garden 'These Four Walls' 123
Hall, Marney and Yarrow, Heather: 'the
  4head garden of dreams' 22
Hallam, Adrian 172, 173
Hampton Court Palace RHS Flower
  Show 48
hard landscaping 100, 102, 170, 204,
  210
hardwood 137
Hedera (ivy) 32
hedging 28, 29, 52, 142, 142, 150
  box 54, 82, 100, 217
  clipped 22, 54, 128, 217
  dark green 76
  hornbeam 46, 47, 216
  tiered 25
  yew (*Taxus baccata*) 120, 126, 127, 148,
  149, 150, 151
Helios 103
Herald, Dean 100, 101
herbaceous planting 137
herbs 63, 176, 177, 181
  how to grow 179, 179
  salad 185
Herring, Andrew 49
Heuchera 72, 167
  'Peach Flambé' 62
Hill, Sue and Peter 22
Hillier Landscapes 49
hornbeam 29, 46, 47, 78, 78, 79, 216
hostas 79, 115
Howarth, Maggy 125
huts
  beach 96
  'rib-cage' timber 95

I
In the grove 148, 149
industrial mesh 28
Iris 54, 71, 113
irises 52
  bearded 17, 53, 54, 56, 67
  orange-bearded 47
ironworks, rustic 94
ivy, climbing (*Hedera*) 32

J
Jekyll, Gertrude 128
juniper 61

K
keys 165
kickboards 28, 145
kitchen garden 183, 184
kitchens, outdoor 83, 100, 101
knapped flint 145

L
Landform Consultants Ltd 217
lantern, Japanese-inspired 195
Laurent-Perrier garden 46, 46-7, 78,
  78-9
lavender 56, 99, 115
lawn turf 62
lemon balm 181
Lennox-Boyd, Arabella 126, 127

Lenti, Paola 151
lettuces 181, 183, 184
Libertia grandiflora 74
lighting 143, 188-201
  aqua dramatics 196, 196, 197
  artworks 209
  case study 200-201
  coloured 191
  freestanding lights 192
  halogen 193, 193
  highlights 194
  illuminating effects 192, 192
  LED lights 117, 171, 193, 193
  light sources 193, 193
  lighting the specific 194, 194, 195
  metal halide 193
  photovoltaic 154, 190
  and reflections 119
  sodium 193
  submerged 120
  techniques 196-7
limestone 31, 88, 149, 150
Limonium platyphyllum 69
Linnaeus, Carl 21, 142
'living' tower 159, 172, 172
loggia 128, 129
logs 31, 101, 155, 159
Lotus corniculatus (bird's foot trefoil) 169
low maintenance gardens 17
lupins 213

M
McVicar, Jekka 179, 185
'magical and mad' gardens 22
maple 129
Marshalls plc 171
Marshalls' Sustainability Garden 170, 171
materials
  bringing the space alive 142, 142
  case studies 148-51
  decking 137, 137
  full on colour 140, 141
  materials up close 136
  metals 134, 135
  pushing boundaries 132
  reusing 158, 159
  thinking outside the box 146, 147
  using glass 143, 143
mats, rubber 28
Matthiola incana 67
Mawson, Thomas 128
Mediterranean style 18, 18, 22
metal 132, 134, 135
  rusting 29
microclimates 168
mini-canal 109
minimalist planting 66, 66, 67
mirrors 126, 204
misting machines 117
mixed planting, and sustainability 154, 160, 168, 169
modernist buildings 94
modernist designs 52
modernist gardens 52, 54, 54, 55
moisture-loving plants 62
moon gate 28, 45, 46, 47
mosaics 38, 125, 140, 141

moss 32, 45
Muehlenbeckia 208
mulch 74, 147, 149, 165
mustard (*Brassica juncea*) 185

N
Nash, Philip 209, 215
native plants 163, 164, 168
naturalistic style 71, 71
Nature Ascending (2009) 163, 213
Nepeta 56
Niwaki 73
Nixon, Philip 145, 216, 217
Nordfjell, Ulf 21
Nymphaea alba 126, 127

O
oaks 63, 138, 139
  fastigiate (columnar) 46, 47
sculpture 150, 151, 151
Oceânico Garden (2008) 199, 200, 200-201
Oda, Mari-Ruth 94
Oenothera macrocarpa 69
orangery 109
oregano (*Origanum vulgare*) 179
Origanum vulgare (oregano) 179
ornamental meadows 53
ornamental plantings, and herbs 179
ornaments 101, 128
Osteospermum 74
Outdoor Room, The 151

P
Packard, Simon 77
palms 58, 61, 137
panels
  glass 143
  white 216, 217
pansies 72, 135
Papaver rhoeas (corn poppy) 56
Pape, Gabriella 77
parsley 187
parties 99, 99
paths 29, 38, 78
  cobbled 31
  cuboid theme 39
  grass 142, 187
  gravel 214
  irregular 46
  lighting 197
  limestone 150
  linear 150
  mosaic 38, 141
  sandstone slabs 39
  slate 126, 127
  square 45
  staggered 45
  in vegetable plots 187
  wet pointing 38
pavilions 150, 151, 201
paving 28, 48, 71, 78, 127, 140, 145, 169
  concrete 43
  differing heights 47
  and ground water levels 154
  Indian sandstone 170, 171
  permeable 103
  stone 101, 128, 137, 171
peonies 39, 148, 149

perennials 63, 148
  herbaceous 46, 53, 68, 168
pergolas 76, 77, 82
Perry, Stuart 123
Perspex 29, 132, 142, 143, 205
pest control 164
Peter Dowle Plants and Gardens 129
pets 108
Phalaris arundinacea 55
Phlomis russeliana 69
Phormium 71
photograph collection 147
Phyllostachys bamboo 127
Phyllostachys iridescens 149
Pinus sylvestris 'Watereri' 61
plant supports 186
planters 29, 72, 72, 73, 74, 132, 132, 134, 135, 140, 143, 147, 155, 181, 185, 197, 216
planting 50-79
  in blocks 54, 54
  case studies 76-9
  coaxing plants to perform 52-3
  colour-themed 62-5, 76
  cottage-garden 52, 54, 54
  diversity in 168, 169
  drought-tolerant 58, 58, 69, 69
  formality and grandeur 60, 61
  layered 63, 63
  marginal 113, 113
  minimalist 66, 66, 67
  modernist 52, 54, 54, 55
  naturalistic style 71, 71
  plant trends 53
plastics 29
Platanus x hispanica 127
play garden 137
Plexiglass 143
plinths 73, 85, 215
pods, sunken white 95
pollution absorption 172
ponds 108, 128
  'black' 106
  edging 113
  and 'grey' water 170
  informal 160
  pond lining 113
  raised 43
pools 100, 157, 160, 172, 173, 216
  copper 159
  lap 107
  ornamental 48
  overflow 113
  raised 217
  square 118
  swimming 106
porches 169
posts, vertical 29
pots 73, 128, 158, 214, 215
  terracotta 74, 99
Potsdam-Bornim sunken garden 76
potting compost 72, 169
preservatives 137
Primula veris (cowslip) 169
primulas 115
projector, outdoor 91
pruning, cloud 73, 73, 78, 79, 79
Prunus 193

laurocerasus 201
Pterocarya fraxinifolia 127

R
railings, iron 28, 36, 36, 44
raised beds 155, 180, 181, 186, 187
Real Rubbish Garden, The (2005) 115
recycling 154, 155, 157, 204, 211
Rhododendron 73
RHS Campaign for School gardening 177
RHS Chelsea Flower Show
  Chelsea style 16-25
  coaxing plants to perform 52-3
  Great Pavilion floral displays 52
  location 113
  massed plantings of one plant type 67
  plant trends 53
  sets the tone for the gardening year 52
rills 106, 125, 172, 173
rocks 113, 126, 127
Rodgersia 61
rodgersias 79
Rolling Stone Landscapes 101
romantic style 17, 17
roofs
  acrylic 94
  green 53, 97, 154, 155, 166, 166, 169, 169, 172, 172, 186
  roof gardens 143
Rosa 'Bobbie James' 77
rosemary 25, 181
roses 17, 52
  climbing 76
runner beans 177, 186

S
sage (*Salvia officinalis*) 167, 179, 181
salad rocket (*Eruca vesicaria* subsp. *sativa*) 185
Salvia 52, 71
  nemorosa
  'Caradonna' 77
  'Ostfriesland' 77
  x *sylvestris* 'Mainacht' 77
salvias 76
sandstone 137, 170, 193
  disc 46, 47
Sarracenia 113
Satureja montana (savory) 179
Savills Garden 145, 216, 216-17
Savills plc 217
savory (*Satureja montana*) 179
scaffold poles/boards 102, 102
Scarpa, Carlo 46
Scenic Blue Design Team 170, 171
Schinus molle 61
screens 18, 28, 29, 36, 138, 142, 142
  dividing 134, 205
  glass 37, 102, 143
  smooth-rendered walls 37
  white 37, 94
sculpture 17, 22, 29, 46, 47, 77, 94, 98, 107, 109, 110, 117, 125, 132, 134, 150, 151, 190, 204, 206, 207
  anchoring sculpture for safety and security 215, 215
  how to position a sculpture 209, 209

illuminating 194
large 205
stone 205
for strong effect 208, 208
seating 17, 21, 29, 76, 82, 84-93, 100, 132, 138, 192
cubed 82
wood block 39
sedge 62
Sedum sp. 166
Sedum telephium 'Purple Emperor' 69
sedums 169
Sempervivum 53, 58, 74
setts
circular 48, 49
grey 43
paving 39, 78, 79
shade 94, 100, 100, 163, 169
shade-tolerant planting 28, 88, 102, 103
shadows 216, 217
Shao Fan 21
shears, swivel-blade hand 73
sheds 82, 169
shrubs 68, 168
and green walls 167
layered planting 63, 63
silhouetting 197
silver birch 71, 190
slabs
limestone 31
paving 197, 216
sandstone 33, 39
slate 126, 127, 159
sofas, outdoor 83, 90, 91, 100, 101
'soft' planting 46, 115
softwood 137
soil conservation 164
soil improvers 154
solar gate 46, 46
solar panels 170, 171
Soleirolia soleirolii 61
spade head sculpture 214
spatial division 100
sphere, dry-stone 209
spotlighting 194, 195, 197, 201
Stachys 69
byzantina 52, 69, 71
stains 137, 149
steel 29, 33, 77, 89, 102, 110, 125, 132, 134, 135, 139, 142, 159, 208
stepping stones 44
steps 28, 30, 31, 91, 138, 139, 193, 194, 197
designing 30-31
Stipa gigantea 47, 53, 54, 71, 216
Stipa tenuissima 47, 67, 69, 200
stone
as an edging material 113
gabions 147
loggia 129
natural 156
paths 38
paving 101, 128, 137, 171
terraces 148
York 28, 125
stonework 100, 101
stormwater retention 173
story-telling 21, 21
strawberries 177, 184

alpine 169
Stuart-Smith, Tom 53, 63, 73, 78, 79
Sturgeon, Andy 137, 143, 150, 151
succulent plants 18, 68, 74, 137
Summer Solstice 186, 186-7
summerhouses 82, 96, 97, 169
'sun beds' 83
sun roses (*Cistus*) 56
sunflowers 183
sustainability 152-73
attracting wildlife 160, 160
case studies 170-73
diversity in planting 168, 169, 169
green roofs and living walls 166, 166, 167, 169, 169
as part of the plan 156, 157
reusing materials 158, 159
statements with 164, 164, 165
sustainable development 154
Swatton, Steven 149
sweet peas 186
sweet Williams 56
swimming pool 106
symmetry 18, 128

T
table runners 99
tables 29, 43, 95, 132
coffee 101
crushed car 147
dining 100, 101
glass-top 100, 100
tanks, zinc 78, 78, 147
Taxus baccata (yew) 76
Telegraph Media Group 77
terraces 148
terracotta 18, 74, 99, 147
urns 205
Thompson, Angus 163, 213
thyme (*Thymus vulgaris*) 169, 179, 181
tiles
glass 195
roofing 159, 171
terracotta 18
timber 132, 132, 137, 138, 139, 145
tomatoes 183
topiary 211
Trachycarpus fortunei 61
trees
apple 181
and diversity in planting 168
fruit 18, 176, 177
layered planting 63
multistemmed 163
olive 41
role in show gardens 52
rows of 60
screening by 100
shade-giving 18, 100
and wildlife 68
trelliswork 28, 29, 82
trompe-l'oeil 204
troughs 21, 78, 110
tulips 142, 169
tyres, planted 165

U
umbellifers 53, 56
University of Sheffield: BUGS project (Biodiversity in Urban Gardens in Sheffield) 154
uplighting 196, 197
urban heat island effect 164
urns 73, 205

V
Van Groeningen, Isabelle 76, 77
vegetables 99, 154, 165, 176, 176, 177, 177, 178, 181, 183, 184, 185, 186, 186
Verbascum 67, 213
phoeniceum 69
Viburnum
opulus 'Roseum' 54
plicatum f. *tomentosum* 'Mariesii' 129
rhytidophyllum 52
vines 68
vortex, swirling 117

W
walkways 102, 109
walls 28, 32, 142
boundary 49, 159
chequerboard 33
coloured 18, 132
concrete column 48
curved 87, 107
decorative, textured 132
divided into sections 32
dry-stone 33
end 94
'living' 102, 103, 166, 167
with moss tracks 32
a 'moving' 33
rammed earth 32, 43, 43, 137
rendered 147, 160
retaining 48, 49, 88, 89, 93, 132
rock 120
small 29
smooth 31, 32, 37, 48, 142
stone 56, 100, 101, 148
timber 91, 95, 139
vertical planting on 53
white-painted 35
wooden dividing 41
washing line 97
washing tub 74
water
absorption 166, 172
and attracting wildlife 170
case studies 126-9
defined role 110
drainage 48
drops for drama 120
edging 113, 113
first steps to water gardening 106-7
focusing water's direction 125
'grey' 102, 159, 170
harvesting 154
irrigation 48, 68, 103, 156, 159, 173
jets 116, 117, 118, 196
levels 48, 49, 129
making water work 106
management 154

movement 116-25
pockets of 163
purification 173
recycling 159, 159
reflections 106, 118-19, 126, 127, 216
simple and effective 108
and steel 135
storage 156, 172
'water wall' 41, 120
water butt 56
water chutes 125
water features 18, 39, 46, 78, 84, 91, 93, 95, 100, 100, 102, 104-29, 143, 190, 197, 204, 208
water hawthorn (*Aponogeton distachyos*) 110
waterfalls 117
watering 72, 169
watering can 56
waterlilies 126, 127, 128, 129
'waves', wooden 107
weeding 169
wheat 68, 186, 187
wheel nuts 165
wheelbarrow 128, 129
Whitehouse, Claire 115
wild flowers 164, 164, 169
wildflower meadows 22
wildlife 21-2, 21, 68, 68, 113, 116, 154, 155, 155, 159, 163, 164, 172, 173, 210, 211
attracting 160, 160
and diversity in planting 168
and gabions 170
and green roofs 169
and living walls 166
wisteria 96
Wisteria sinensis 77
Witan Wisdom Garden (2009) 87
wood offcuts 132
Wormcast Company 129

Y
Yarrow, Heather 22
yew (*Taxus baccata*) 25, 76, 76, 120, 126, 127, 148, 149, 150, 151
York stone 28, 125
Yorkshire Water 173
Yucca rostrata 62

Z
Zantedeschia 62, 165

ACKNOWLEDGEMENTS

At the heart of this book is an immense gratitude to all those people who have created, and continue to create, gardens at the RHS Chelsea Flower Show. This book focuses primarily on the show from 2004 to 2009, but such recognition and thanks span the show's history. Without the vision, skill, enthusiasm and energy of the exhibitors – plus the seemless organisation by the RHS shows department – the RHS Chelsea Flower Show wouldn't be able to lead the way in garden design and plantsmanship.

Garden designers, landscape architects, nurserymen, landscape contractors, lighting engineers, sculptors, water specialists, educational establishments...the list of people involved is endless. Yet by coming together in the name of gardens and horticulture, their collective skills inspire and inform thousands of us each year. It may seem obvious, but without them this book really wouldn't be possible.

In addition, thanks goes to the team at the RHS books department, especially Rae Spencer Jones and her tireless support during the development and writing of this book. Her guidance has been much appreciated, and her judgement hard to fault. So too, many thanks to publishers Mitchell Beazley – on the editing side Helen Griffin, Joanne Wilson and Joanna Chisholm, and on the design side Juliette Norsworthy and Lizzie Ballantyne.

Together, I hope we have made a book that continues to keep the spirit of Chelsea alive, helping home gardeners to get the most out of their private space.

**Chris Young, Ketton, Lincolnshire
October 2009**

PHOTOGRAPHY CREDITS